How to Live Forever ...Without Being Religious

by Ray Comfort

Bridge-Logos

Orlando, Florida 82822

Bridge-Logos
Orlando, FL 82822 USA

How to Live Forever ... Without Being Religious
by Ray Comfort

Printed in the United States of America.

Library of Congress Catalog Card Number: 2007927207
International Standard Book Number: 978-0-88270-425-8 (Large Print)
978-0-88270-163-9 (Pocket size)

Scriptures in the book are from *The Evidence Bible*

G616.316.N.m705.35250

CONTENTS

Introduction

A man in a rowboat once found himself caught in fast-moving water, heading for massive waterfall with jagged rocks 150 feet below. A passerby saw him rowing against the current, but his efforts were futile. Minute by minute he was drawn closer and closer to the roaring falls. The man ran to his car, grabbed a rope from the trunk and threw it to the boat. When it fell across the bow, he screamed, "Grab the rope. I will pull you to the shore!" He couldn't believe his eyes. The man took no notice. He just kept rowing frantically against the current, until he was sucked over the falls to his death.

Therein lies the difference between being a Christian and being religious, but before we look closer at that issue, let me explain what happened to a friend of mine. His name is Danny. When he told me that he once went to prison for failing to pay parking tickets, I asked, "*Why didn't you just pay them?*"

He answered, "They were just 'parking tickets;' it was no big deal."

Then he told me that the police arrived at his home at 4:00 AM, put him in a big black bus and took him to Los Angeles County courts. As he stood before the judge, he said, "Your honor, I brought $700 with me to pay the tickets and to cover the court costs."

The judge said, "Mr. Goodall, I'm going to save you all that money. *You are going to jail!*"

Danny was terrified.

His big mistake was that he trivialized his crimes by thinking that they were "just" parking tickets, and so he deceived himself. Had he known the judge's ruling (that he would go to prison), he would have immediately made things right between himself and the law.

Most of us realize that we have broken God's Law—the Ten Commandments, but it's no big deal. So, let me ask you a few questions about the Law you have broken and see if it is a big deal.

Have you ever lied? You say, "Yes. But they were only white lies. They were nothing serious."

Have you ever stolen something? You say, "Yes, but only little things."

Can you see what you are doing? You are *trivializing* your crimes, and like Danny, you *will* deceive yourself. What you are doing is saying that you haven't actually "sinned." But the Bible warns, "He who says he has no sin *deceives* himself." The truth is that if you have lied, then you are a liar. If you have stolen *anything* (the value of the item stolen is irrelevant), you are a thief.

What you need to hear is the judge's ruling for lying and stealing. Here it is: *"All liars will have their part in the lake of fire"* (Revelation 21:8). *All* liars go to Hell.

You say, "I don't believe in Hell." That's like my friend saying to the judge "I don't believe in jail." What we believe or don't believe doesn't change realities. No thief will enter Heaven. Not one (1 Corinthians 6:9).

Now look at this: Jesus said, *"Whoever looks at a woman to lust for her has already committed adultery with her in his heart"* (Matthew 5:28). Have you ever looked with lust? Then you have committed adultery as far as God is concerned. Have you used God's name in vain? If you have, then you have used His holy name as a cuss word to express disgust. That's called "blasphemy," and it's very serious in God's sight.

So if you have been honest enough to admit that you have broken those Commandments, you are a self-admitted lying, thieving, blasphemous adulterer at heart. If God gives you justice on Judgment Day, you will be guilty and end up in Hell. Think of it—if you died right now, you would end up in Hell, forever. So what are you going to do? How can you make things right between you and the Law?

The Bible tells us that you cannot "do" anything. But God Himself did something wonderful to save you from death and

Hell. He became a person in Jesus Christ, and suffered and died in your place. He paid the fine in His life's blood for the crimes that you committed: "God demonstrates His own love toward us, in that while we were still sinners, Christ died for us." Then He rose from the dead and defeated death.

Now here's the difference between being religious and being a Christian. There are millions of people on this earth who have never seen the serious nature of sin. They are in the dark about the Judge's ruling. They have no idea that they will end up in Hell for crimes that they consider trivial. They know that they have to face God after death, but they think that their religious works (like Danny with his $700) will buy their way out of any trouble in which they may find themselves. And as long as they trivialize their sin, they will deceive themselves into thinking that they can work their way into Heaven by their religious works. But it is as futile as the man who tried to row against the river until he went over the falls.

God Himself has thrown us a rope in Jesus Christ. He is the only One who can save us from death and Hell. But we must let go of our own efforts to save ourselves and take hold of the rope. The moment we cease our own religious "rowing" and have faith in Jesus, we find peace with God. The Bible says, *"For by grace are you saved through faith, and that not of yourselves. It is the gift of God, not of works, least any man boast"* (Ephesians 2:8-9).

To be saved, you must repent and then trust in the Savior. If you do that, God will forgive you and grant you eternal life. He will dismiss your case. He will commute your death sentence and allow you to live. This is called being "born again." Jesus said, *"Unless one is born again, he cannot see the kingdom of God"* (John 3:3). If you are not born again, you cannot enter Heaven. So, please pray something like this:

"Dear God, I confess I am a sinner. Thank You that Jesus took my punishment upon Himself when He died on the Cross for my sins, and then rose from the dead, defeating death. Today, I repent and place my trust in Jesus Christ alone for my salvation. In Jesus' name I pray. Amen."

Now flip over in this publication to John 14:21 and read it. Then determine to read your Bible daily and obey what you read.

The next few pages contain *Save Yourself Some Pain*. These are important principles for Christian growth. Then you will find *The Gospel of John* taken directly from *The Evidence Bible*. For more information about this Bible, see the last pages of this publication.

Thank you for taking the time to read this.

God bless you,
Ray Comfort.

Save Yourself Some Pain

It is my sincere hope that you have made peace with God. Becoming a Christian is the most incredible event that will ever take place in your life. If you have obeyed the Gospel by turning from your sins and placing your trust in Jesus Christ, you have found everlasting life! Be assured, God will never leave you nor forsake you. He has brought you this far and He will complete the wonderful work He has begun in you. God knows your every thought, your every care, and your deepest concerns.

Let's look at some of those possible concerns. First, and of primary concern, is: Do you have "assurance" of your salvation?

We are told to "make your calling and election sure" (2 Peter 1:10, emphasis added), so let's go through a short "checklist" to make sure that you are truly saved in the biblical sense:

- Are you aware that God became flesh in the person of Jesus Christ (1 Timothy 3:16), and that He died for the sins of the world?
- Did you come to the Savior because you had sinned against God?
- Did you "repent" and put your faith (trust) in Jesus?
- Are you convinced that He suffered and died on the cross for your sins, and that He rose again on the third day?

Following are additional important principles that can save you a great deal of pain.

1. DAILY NUTRITION
Feeding on the Word

A healthy baby has a healthy appetite. If you have truly been "born" of the Spirit of God, you will have a healthy appetite. We are told, "As newborn babes, desire the pure milk of the word, that you may grow thereby" (1 Peter 2:2). Feed yourself daily without fail. Job said, "I have treasured the words of His mouth more than my necessary food" (Job 23:12). The more you eat, the quicker you will grow, and the less bruising you will have. Speed up the process and save yourself some pain—vow to read God's Word every day without fail. Say to yourself, "No Bible, no breakfast. No read, no feed." Be like Job, and put your Bible before your belly. If you do that, God promises that you will be like a fruitful, strong, and healthy tree (see Psalm 1). Each day, find somewhere quiet and thoroughly soak your soul in the Word of God.

There may be times when you read through its pages with great enthusiasm, and other times when it seems dry and even boring. But food profits your body whether you enjoy it or not.

As a child, you no doubt ate desserts with great enthusiasm. Perhaps vegetables weren't so exciting. If you were a normal child, you probably had to be encouraged to eat them at first. Then, as you matured in life, you learned to discipline yourself to eat vegetables. This is because they physically benefit you, even though they may not bring pleasure to your taste buds.

2. FAITH
Elevators Can Let You Down

When a young man once said to me, "I find it hard to believe some of the things in the Bible," I smiled and asked, "What's your name?"

When he said, "Paul," I casually answered, "I don't believe you." He looked at me questioningly.

I repeated, "What's your name?"

Again he said, "Paul." And again I answered, "I don't believe you."

Then I asked, "Where do you live?"

When he told me, I said, "I don't believe that either."

His reaction, understandably, was anger.

I said, "You look a little upset. Do you know why? You're upset because I didn't believe what you told me. If you tell me that your name is Paul, and I say, 'I don't believe you,' it means that I think you are a liar. You are trying to deceive me by telling me your name is Paul, when it's not."

Then I told him that if he, a mere man, felt insulted by my lack of faith in his word, how much more does he insult Almighty God by refusing to believe His Word. In doing so, he was saying that God isn't worth trusting—that He is a liar and a deceiver. The Bible says, "He who does not believe God has made Him a liar" (1 John 5:10). It also says, "Beware, brethren, lest there be in any of you an evil heart of unbelief ..." (Hebrews 3:12).

Martin Luther said, "What greater insult ... can there be to God, than not to believe His promises."

I have heard people say, "But I just find it hard to have faith in God," not realizing the implications of their words. These are the same people who accept the daily weather forecast, believe the newspapers, and trust their lives to a pilot they have never seen whenever they board a plane. We exercise faith every day. We rely on our cars' brakes. We trust history books, medical books, and elevators. Yet elevators can let us down. History books can be wrong. Planes can crash. How much more then should we trust the sure and true promises of Almighty God? He will never let us down ... if we trust Him.

Cynics argue, "You can't trust the Bible—it's full of mistakes."

It is. The first mistake was when man rejected God. The Scriptures show men and women making the same tragic mistakes again and again. It's also full of what seem to be contradictions.

3

For example, the Scriptures tell us, "With God, nothing shall be impossible" (Luke 1:37). There is nothing Almighty God can't do. Yet we are also told that it is "impossible for God to lie" (Hebrews 6:18). So there is something God cannot do! Isn't that an obvious "mistake" in the Bible? The answer to this dilemma is found in the lowly worm.

Do you know that it would be impossible for me to eat worms? I once saw a man on TV butter his toast, then pour on a can of live, fat, wriggling, blood-filled worms. He carefully took a knife and fork, cut into his moving meal, and ate it. It made me feel sick. It was disgusting. The thought of chewing cold, live worms is so repulsive, so distasteful that I can candidly say it would be impossible for me to eat them, although I have seen it done. It is so abhorrent that I draw on the strength of the word, "impossible," to substantiate my claim.

Lying, deception, bearing false witness, etc., are so repulsive to God, so disgusting to Him, so against His holy character that the Scriptures draw on the strength of the word, "impossible," to substantiate the claim. He cannot, could not, and would not lie. That means, in a world where we are continually let down, we can totally rely on, trust in, and count on His promises. They are sure, certain, indisputable, true, trustworthy, reliable, faithful, unfailing, dependable, and steadfast, and an anchor for the soul. In other words, you can truly believe them, and because of that, you can throw yourself blindfolded and without reserve into His mighty hands. He will never, ever let you down. Do you believe that?

3. EVANGELISM
Our Most Sobering Task

Late in December 1996, a large family gathered in Los Angeles for a joyous Christmas. There were so many gathered that night, five of the children slept in the converted garage, kept warm during the night by an electric heater placed near the door. During the early hours of the morning, the heater suddenly burst into flames, blocking the doorway. In seconds the room became a blazing inferno. A frantic 911 call revealed the unspeakable terror as one of the children could be heard screaming, "I'm on fire!" The distraught father rushed into the flames to try to save his beloved children, receiving burns to 50 percent of his body. Tragically, all five children burned to death. They died because steel bars on the windows had thwarted their escape. There was only one door, and it was blocked by the flames.

Imagine you are back in time, just minutes before the heater burst into flames. You peer through the darkness at the peaceful sight of five sleeping youngsters, knowing that at any moment the room will erupt into an inferno and burn the flesh of horrified children. Can you in good conscience walk away? No! You must awaken them, and warn them to run from that deathtrap! If you don't warn them, you are breaking the law.

The world sleeps peacefully in the darkness of ignorance. There is only one Door by which they may escape death. The steel bars of sin prevent their salvation, and at the same time call for the flames of eternal justice.

What a fearful thing Judgment Day will be! The fires of the wrath of Almighty God will burn for eternity. The Church has been entrusted with the task of awakening people before it's too late. We cannot turn our backs and walk away in complacency. Think of how the father ran into the flames. His love knew no bounds.

Our devotion to the sober task God has given us will be in direct proportion to our love for the lost. There are only a few who run headlong into the flames to warn them to flee (Luke 10:2). Please be one of them. We really have no choice. The apostle Paul said, "Woe is me if I do not preach the gospel!" (1 Corinthians 9:16).

If you and I ignore a drowning child and let him die when we had the ability to save him, we are guilty of the crime of "depraved indifference." God forbid that any Christian should be guilty of that crime when it comes to those around us who are perishing. We have an obligation to reach out to them.

The "Prince of Preachers," Charles Spurgeon, said, "Have you no wish for others to be saved? Then you are not saved yourself. Be sure of that."

A Christian cannot be apathetic about the salvation of the world. The love of God in him will motivate him to seek and save all who are lost. You probably have a limited amount of time after your conversion to impact your unsaved friends and family with the gospel. After the initial shock of your conversion, they will put you in a neat little ribbon-tied box, and keep you at arm's length. So it's important that you take advantage of the short time you have while you still have their ears[3].

Here's some advice that may save you a great deal of grief. As a new Christian, I did almost irreparable damage by acting like a wild bull in a crystal showroom. I bullied my mom, my dad, and many of my friends into making a "decision for Christ." I was sincere, zealous, loving, kind, and stupid. I didn't understand that salvation doesn't come through making a "decision," but through repentance, and that repentance is God-given (2 Timothy 2:25).

The Bible teaches that no one can come to the Son unless the Father "draws" him (John 6:44). If you are able to get a "decision," but the person has no conviction of sin, you will almost certainly end up with a stillborn on your hands.

In my "zeal without knowledge," I actually inoculated the very ones I was so desperately trying to reach. There is nothing more important to you than the salvation of your loved ones, and you don't want to blow it. If you do, you may find that you don't have a second chance. Fervently pray for them, asking God for their salvation. Let them see your faith. Let them feel your kindness, your genuine love, and your gentleness. Buy gifts for no reason. Do chores when you are not asked to. Go the extra mile.

Put yourself in their position. You know that you have found everlasting life—death has lost its sting! Your joy is unspeakable. But as far as they are concerned, you've been brainwashed and have become part of a weird sect. So your loving actions will speak more loudly than ten thousand eloquent sermons. For this reason, you should avoid verbal confrontation until you have knowledge that will guide your zeal. Pray for wisdom and for sensitivity to God's timing. You may have only one shot, so make it count. Keep your cool. If you don't, you may end up with a lifetime of regret.

Believe me. It is better to hear a loved one or a close friend say, "Tell me about your faith in Jesus Christ," rather than you saying, "Sit down. I want to talk to you."

Continue to persevere in prayer for them, that God would open their eyes to the truth.

Remember also that you have the sobering responsibility of speaking to other people's loved ones. Perhaps another Christian has prayed earnestly that God would use a faithful witness to speak to his beloved mom or dad, and you are that answer to prayer. You are the true and faithful witness God wants to use.

We should share our faith with others whenever we can. The Bible says that there are only two times we should do this: "in season and out of season" (2 Timothy 4:2). The apostle Paul pleaded for prayer for his own personal witness. He said, "[Pray] for me, that utterance may be given to me, that I may open my mouth boldly to make known the mystery of the gospel, for which I am an ambassador in chains; that in it I may speak boldly, as I ought to speak" (Ephesians 6:19, 20).

Never lose sight of the world and all its pains. Keep the fate of the ungodly before your eyes. Too many of us settle down on a padded pew and become introverted. Our world becomes a monastery without walls. Our friends are confined solely to those within the Church, when Jesus was the "friend of sinners." So take the time to deliberately befriend the lost for the sake of their salvation. Remember that each and every person who dies in his sins has an appointment with the Judge of the Universe. Hell opens wide its terrible jaws. There is no more sobering task than to be entrusted with the gospel of salvation—working with God for the eternal wellbeing of dying humanity.

7

The Key

Many Christians have thought, There must be a key to reaching the lost. There is—and it's rusty through lack of use. The Bible does actually call it "the key," and its purpose is to bring us to Christ, to unlock the Door of the Savior (see John 10:9). Much of the Church still doesn't even know it exists. Not only is it biblical, but also it can be shown through history that the Church used it to unlock the doors of revival.

The problem is that it was lost around the turn of the twentieth century. Keys have a way of getting lost. Jesus used it. So did Paul (Romans 3:19, 20) and James (James 2:10). Stephen used it when he preached (Acts 7:53). Peter found that it had been used to open the door to release 3,000 imprisoned souls on the Day of Pentecost. Jesus said that the lawyers had "taken away" the key, and had even refused to use it to let people enter into the Kingdom of God (Luke 11:52). The Pharisees didn't take it away; instead, they bent it out of shape so that it wouldn't do its work (Mark 7:8). Jesus returned it to its true shape, just as the Scriptures prophesied that He would do (Isaiah 42:21).

Satan has tried to prejudice the modern Church against the key. He has maligned it, misused it, twisted it, and, of course, hidden it—he hates it because of what it does.

Perhaps you are wondering what this key is. I will tell you. All I ask is that you set aside your traditions and prejudices and look at what God's Word says on the subject. In Acts 28:23 the Bible tells us that Paul sought to persuade his hearers "concerning Jesus, both out of the law of Moses, and out of the prophets." Here we have two effective means of persuading the unsaved "concerning Jesus."

Let's first look at how the prophets can help persuade sinners concerning Jesus. Fulfilled prophecy proves the inspiration of Scripture. The predictions of the prophets present a powerful case for the inspiration of the Bible. Any skeptic who reads the prophetic words of Isaiah, Ezekiel, Joel, etc., or the words of Jesus in Matthew 24 cannot but be challenged that this is no ordinary book.

The other means by which Paul persuaded sinners concerning Jesus was "out of the law of Moses." We are told that the Law of Moses is good if it is used lawfully (1 Timothy 1:8). It was given by God as a "tutor" to bring us to Christ (Galatians 3:24). Paul wrote that he "would not have known sin except through the law" (Romans 7:7). The Law of God (the Ten Commandments) is evidently the "key of knowledge" of which Jesus spoke in Luke 11:52. He was speaking to "lawyers"—those who should have been teaching God's Law so that sinners would receive the "knowledge of sin," and thus recognize their need for the Savior.

Prophecy speaks to the intellect of the sinner, while the Law speaks to his conscience. One produces faith in the Word of God; the other brings knowledge of sin in the heart of the sinner.

The Law is the God-given "key" to unlock the Door of salvation. You may have noticed that I used this principle in this book.

4. PRAYER
"Wait for a Minute"

As I mentioned earlier in this book, God always answers prayer. Sometimes He says, "Yes." Sometimes He says, "No." And sometimes He says, "Wait for a minute." And since God is outside the dimension of time, a thousand years is the same as a day to Him (see 2 Peter 3:8)—which could mean a ten-year wait for us. So ask in faith, but rest in peace-filled patience.

Surveys show that more than 90 percent of Americans pray daily. No doubt they pray for health, wealth, happiness, etc. They also pray when Grandma gets sick, so when Grandma doesn't get better (or dies), many end up disillusioned or bitter. This is because they don't understand what the Bible says about prayer. It teaches, among other things, that our sin will keep God from even hearing our prayers (Psalm 66:18), and that if we pray with doubt, we will not get an answer (James 1:6, 7). Here's how to be heard:

- Pray with faith (Hebrews 11:6).
- Pray with clean hands and a pure heart (Psalm 24:3, 4).
- Pray genuine heartfelt prayers, rather than vain repetitions (Matthew 6:7).
- Make sure you are praying to the God revealed in the Scriptures (Exodus 20:3–6).

How to "pray with faith." If someone says to you, "You have great faith in God," they may think they are paying you a compliment. But they aren't—the compliment is to God. For example, if I said, "I'm a man of great faith in my doctor," it's actually the doctor I'm complimenting. If I have great faith in him, it means that I see him as being a man of integrity, a man of great ability; he is trustworthy. I give "glory" to the man through my faith in him.

The Bible says that Abraham "did not waver at the promise of God through unbelief, but was strengthened in faith, giving glory to God, and being fully convinced that what He had promised He was also able to perform" (Romans 4:20, 21). Abraham was a man of great faith in God. Remember, that is not a compliment to Abraham. He merely caught a glimpse of God's incredible ability, His impeccable integrity, and His wonderful faithfulness to keep every promise He makes. Abraham's faith gave "glory" to a faithful God.

As far as God is concerned, if you belong to Jesus, you are a VIP. You can boldly come before the throne of grace (Hebrews 4:16). You have access to the King because you are the son or daughter of the King. When you were a child, did you have to grovel to get your needs met by your mom or dad? I hope not. So, when you pray, don't say, "Oh, God, I hope you will supply my needs." Instead, say something like:

"Father, thank You that You keep every promise You make. Your Word says that you will supply all my needs according to Your riches in glory by Christ Jesus [Philippians 4:19].

Therefore, I thank You that You will do this thing for my family. I ask this in the wonderful name of Jesus. Amen."

The great missionary, Hudson Taylor, said, "The prayer power has never been tried to its full capacity. If we want to see Divine power wrought in the place of weakness, failure, and disappointment, let us answer God's standing challenge, 'Call unto me, and I will answer you, and show you great and mighty things of which you know not of.'"

How to get "clean hands and a pure heart." Simply confess your sins to God through Jesus Christ, whose blood cleanses us from all our sin (1 John 1:7–9). When you confess them to God through Jesus, God not only forgives your every sin, but He promises to forget them (Hebrews 8:12). He will count it as though you had never sinned in the first place. He will make you pure in His sight—sinless. He will even "purge" your conscience, so that you will no longer have that sense of guilt that you sinned. That's why you need to soak yourself in Holy Scripture; read the letters to the churches and see the wonderful things God has done for us through the cross of Calvary. If you don't bother to read the "will," you won't have any idea what has been given to you.

How to pray "genuine heartfelt prayers." Simply keep yourself in the love of God. If the love of God is in you, you will never pray hypocritical or selfish prayers. In fact, you won't have to pray selfish prayers if you have a heart of love, because when your prayer-life is pleasing to God, He will reward you openly (Matthew 6:6). Just talk to your heavenly Father as candidly and intimately as a young child, nestled on Daddy's lap, would talk to his earthly father. How would you feel if every day your child pulled out a pre-written statement to dryly recite to you, rather than poured out the events and emotions of that day? God wants to hear from your heart.

How to know you're praying to "the God revealed in Scripture."
Study the Bible. Don't accept the image of God portrayed by the world, even though it appeals to the natural mind. A loving, kind fatherly-figure with no sense of justice or truth appeals to guilty sinners. Look to the thunderings and lightnings of Mount Sinai. Gaze at Jesus on the cross of Calvary—hanging in unspeakable agony because of the justice of a holy God. Such thoughts tend to banish idolatry.

5. WARFARE
Praise the Lord and Pass the Ammunition

When you became a Christian, you stepped right into the heat of an age-old battle. You now have a threefold enemy: the world, the flesh, and the devil. Let's look at these three resistant enemies.

Our first enemy is the world. When the Bible speaks of the "world" in this context, it is referring to the sinful, rebellious, world system. This is the world that loves the darkness and hates the light (John 3:20), and is governed by the "prince of the power of the air" (Ephesians 2:2).

The Bible says that the Christian has escaped the corruption that is in the world through lust. "Lust" is unlawful desire, and is the life's blood of the world—whether it be the lust for sexual sin, for power, for money, or for material things. Lust is a monster that will never be gratified, so don't feed it. It will grow bigger and bigger until it weighs heavy upon your back, and will be the death of you (James 1:15).

There is nothing wrong with sex, power, money, or material things, but when desire for these becomes predominant, it becomes idolatry (Colossians 3:5). We are told, "Do not love the world or the things in the world. If anyone loves the world, the love of the Father is not in him," and, "Whoever therefore wants to be a friend of the world makes himself an enemy of God" (1 John 2:15; James 4:4).

The second enemy is the devil. As we have seen, he is known as the "god of this age" (2 Corinthians 4:4). He was your spiritual father before you joined the family of God (John 8:44, Ephesians 2:2). Jesus called the devil a thief who came to steal, kill, and destroy (John 10:10). The way to overcome him and his demons is to make sure you are outfitted with the spiritual armor of God listed in Ephesians 6:10–20. Become intimately familiar with it. Sleep in it. Never take it off. Bind the sword to your hand so you never lose its grip. The reason for this brings us to the third enemy.

The third enemy is what the Bible calls the "flesh." This is your sinful nature. The domain for the battle is your mind. If you have a mind to, you will be attracted to the world and all its sin. The mind is the control panel for the eyes and the ears, the center of your appetites.

All sin begins in the "heart" (Proverbs 4:23; Matthew 15:19). We think of sin before we commit it. The Bible warns that lust brings forth sin, and sin, when it's conceived, brings forth death.

Every day of life, we have a choice. To sin or not to sin—that is the question. The answer to the question of sin is to have the fear of God. If you don't fear God, you will sin to your sinful heart's delight. Did you know that God kills people? He killed a man for what he did sexually (Genesis 38:9, 10), killed another man for being greedy (Luke 12:15–21), and killed a husband and wife for telling one lie (Acts 5:1–10).

Knowledge of God's goodness—His righteous judgments against evil—should put the fear of God in us and help us not to indulge in sin. If we know that the eye of the Lord is in every place beholding the evil and the good, and that He will bring every work to judgment, we will live accordingly.

Such weighty thoughts are valuable, for "by the fear of the LORD one departs from evil" (Proverbs 16:6). Jesus said, "And I say to you, My friends, do not be afraid of those who kill the body, and after that have no more that they can do. But I will show you whom you should fear: Fear Him who, after He has killed, has power to cast into hell; yes, I say to you, fear Him!" (Luke 12:4, 5)

6. FELLOWSHIP
Flutter by Butterfly

Pray about where you should fellowship. Make sure the place you select as your church home calls sin what it is—sin. Do they believe the promises of God? Are they loving? Does the pastor treat his wife with respect? Is he a man of the Word? Does he have a humble heart and a gentle spirit? Listen closely to his teaching. It should glorify God, magnify Jesus, and edify the believer.

One evidence that you have been truly saved is that you will have a love for other Christians (1 John 3:14). You will want to fellowship with them. The old saying that "birds of a feather flock together" is true of Christians. You gather together for the breaking of bread (communion), for teaching from the Word, and for fellowship. You share the same inspirations, illuminations, inclinations, temptations, aspirations, motivations, and perspirations—you are working together for the same thing: the furtherance of the Kingdom of God on earth. This is why you attend church—not because you have to, but because you want to.

Don't become a "spiritual butterfly." Send your roots down. If you are flitting from church to church, how will your pastor know what type of food you are digesting? We are told that your shepherd is accountable to God for you (Hebrews 13:17), so make yourself known to your pastor. Pray for him regularly. Pray also for his wife, his family, and the church leaders.

Being a pastor is no easy task. Most people don't realize how many hours it takes to prepare a fresh sermon each week. They don't appreciate the time spent in prayer and in the study of the Word. If the pastor makes the same joke twice or shares something he has shared before, remember he's human. So give him a great deal of grace and double honor.

Never murmur about him. If you don't like something he has said, pray about it; then leave the issue with God. If that doesn't satisfy you, leave the church rather than divide it through murmuring and complaining. A woman once spread some hot gossip about a local pastor. What he had supposedly done became common knowledge around town. Then she found that what she had heard wasn't true. She gallantly went to the pastor and asked for his forgiveness. The pastor forgave her, but then told her to take a pillow full of tiny feathers to a corner of the town, and in high winds, shake the feathers out. Then he told her to try to pick up every feather. He explained that the damage had already been done. She had destroyed his good reputation, and trying to repair the damage was like trying to pick up feathers in high winds.

The Bible says that there is life and death in the power of the tongue (Proverbs 18:21). We can kill or make something alive with our words. The Scriptures also reveal that God hates those who cause division among believers (Proverbs 6:16). Pray with the psalmist, "Set a guard, O LORD, over my mouth; keep watch over the door of my lips" (Psalm 141:3).

Remember the old saying, "He who gossips to you will gossip about you."

7. THANKSGIVING
Do the Right Thing

For the Christian, every day should be Thanksgiving Day. We should be thankful even in the midst of problems. The apostle Paul said, "I am exceedingly joyful in all our tribulation" (2 Corinthians 7:4). He knew that God was working all things together for his good, even though he was going through trials (Romans 8:28).

Problems will come your way. God will see to it personally that you grow as a Christian. He will allow storms in your life in order to send your roots deep into the soil of His Word. We also pray more in the midst of problems. It's been well said that you will see more from your knees than on your tiptoes.

15

A man once watched a butterfly struggling to get out of its cocoon. In an effort to help it, he took a razor blade and carefully slit the edge of the cocoon. The butterfly escaped from its problem—and immediately died. It is God's way to have the butterfly struggle. It is the struggle that causes its tiny heart to beat fast and to send the life's blood into its wings. Trials have their purpose. They make us struggle—they bring us to our knees. They are the cocoons in which we often find ourselves. It is there that the life's blood of faith in God helps us spread our wings.

Faith and thanksgiving are close friends. If you have faith in God, you will be thankful because you know His loving hand is upon you, even though you are in a lion's den. That will give you a deep sense of joy, and joy is the barometer of the depth of faith you have in God.

Let me give you an example. Imagine that I said I'd give you one million dollars if you sent me an email. Of course, you don't believe I would do that, but imagine that you did. Imagine if you knew 1,000 people who had sent me an email, and every one received their million dollars—no strings attached. More than that, you actually called me, and I assured you personally that I would keep my word. If you believed me, wouldn't you have joy? If you didn't believe me—no joy. The amount of joy you have would be a barometer of how much you believed my promise.

We have so much for which to be thankful. God has given us "exceedingly great and precious promises" that are "more to be desired than gold." Do yourself a big favor: believe those promises, thank God continually for them, and "let your joy be full."

8. WATER BAPTISM
Sprinkle or Immerse?

The Bible says, "Repent, and let every one of you be baptized in the name of Jesus Christ for the remission of sins ..." (Acts 2:38). There is no question about whether or not you should be baptized. The questions are how, when, and by whom?

It would seem clear from Scripture that those who were baptized were fully immersed in water. Here's one reason why: "Now John also was baptizing in Aenon near Salim, because there was much water there" (John 3:23). If John were merely sprinkling believers, he would have needed only a cupful of water. Baptism by immersion pictures our death to sin, burial, and resurrection to new life in Christ (see Romans 6:4, Colossians 2:12).

The Philippian jailer and his family were baptized at midnight, the same hour they believed. The Ethiopian eunuch was baptized as soon as he believed (Acts 8:35–37), as was Paul (Acts 9:17, 18). Baptism is a step of obedience, and God blesses our obedience.

So what are you waiting for? Who should baptize you? It is clear from Scripture that other believers have the privilege, but check with your pastor; he may want the honor himself.

9. TITHING
The Final Frontier

It was once said that the wallet is the "last frontier." It is the final area to be conquered—the last thing that comes to God in surrender. Jesus spoke much about money. He said that we cannot serve God and mammon (Matthew 6:24). The word, mammon, was the common Aramaic word for "riches," which is akin to a Hebrew word signifying "that which is to be trusted." In other words, we cannot trust God and money. Either money is our source of life, our great love, our joy, our sense of security, the supplier of our needs—or God is.

When you open your purse or wallet, give generously and regularly to your local church. Give because you want to, not because you have to. **"God loves a cheerful giver"** (2 Corinthians 9:7), so learn to hold your money with a loose hand.

10. TROUBLESHOOTING
Cults, Atheists, Skeptics

If you know the Lord, nothing will shake your faith. It is true that the man with an experience is not at the mercy of a man with an argument. If you are converted, and the Holy Spirit "bears witness" that you are a child of God (Romans 8:16), you will never be shaken by a skeptic.

When cults tell you that you must acknowledge God's name to be saved, that you must worship on a certain day, or that you must be baptized by an elder of their church, don't panic. Merely go back to the Instruction Manual. The Bible has all the answers, and searching them out will make you grow. If you feel intimidated by atheists—if you think they are "intellectuals"—read my book, God Doesn't Believe in Atheists. It will reveal that they are the opposite. It will also show you how to prove God's existence, and also prove that the "atheist" doesn't exist.

Finally, the way to prevent sporting injury and pain is to keep yourself fit. Exercise. The apostle Paul kept fit through exercise. He said, "Herein do I exercise myself, to always have a conscience void of offense toward God, and toward men" (Acts 24:16, KJV). Do the same. Listen to the voice of your conscience. It's your friend, not your enemy. Remember these words of Solomon: "Fear God and keep His commandments, for this is the whole duty of man. For God will bring every work into judgment, including every secret thing, whether it is good or whether it is evil" (Ecclesiastes 12:13, 14). Keep the Day of Judgment before your eyes. On that Day, you will be glad that you cultivated a tender conscience.

I hope these principles have been helpful and that they will some day save you some pain.

The Book of
JOHN

John

Chapter 1

In the beginning was the Word, and the Word was with God, and the Word was God.

2   The same was in the beginning with God.

3   All things were made by him; and without him was not any thing made that was made.

4   In him was life; and the life was the light of men.

5   And the light shines in darkness; and the darkness comprehended it not.

1:3,4   Rejection of the Bible's account of creation as given in the Book of Genesis could rightly be called "Genecide," because it eradicated man's purpose of existence and left a whole generation with no certainty as to its beginning. Consequently, theories and tales of our origin have crept like primeval slime from the minds of those who don't know God. This intellectual genocide has given the godless a temporary license to labor to the extremes of their imagination, giving birth to painful conjecture of human beginnings. They speak in speculation, the uncertain language of those who drift aimlessly across the endless sea of secular philosophy.

The Scriptures, on the other hand, deal only with truth and certainty. They talk of fact, reality, and purpose for man's existence. The darkness of the raging sea of futility retreats where the lighthouse of Genesis begins.

1:9   On the Day of Judgment no one can plead ignorance. God has given light to every man. (See also 2 Corinthians 4:6.)

1:11   Messianic prophecy fulfilled: "He is despised and rejected of men; a man of sorrows, and acquainted with grief: and we hid as it were our faces from him; he was despised, and we esteemed him not" (Isaiah 53:3). See John 1:32 comment.

1:13   New birth—its necessity for salvation: See John 3:7.

1:13 The "Sinner's Prayer"— To Pray or Not To Pray?

The question often arises about what a Christian should do if someone is repentant. Should we lead him in what's commonly called a "sinner's prayer" or simply instruct him to seek after God? Perhaps the answer comes by looking to the natural realm. As long as there are no complications when a child is born, all the doctor needs to do is guide the head. The same applies spiritually. When someone is "born of God," all we need to do is guide the head—make sure that they understand what they are doing.

Philip the evangelist did this with the Ethiopian eunuch. He asked him, "Do you understand what you read?" (Acts 8:30). In the parable of the sower, the true convert (the "good soil" hearer) is he who hears "and understands." This understanding comes by the Law in the hand of the Spirit (Romans 7:7). If a sinner is ready for the Savior, it is because he has been drawn by the Holy Spirit (John 6:44). This is why we must be careful to allow the Holy Spirit to do His work and not rush in where angels fear to tread. Praying a sinner's prayer with someone who isn't genuinely repentant may leave you with a stillborn in your hands. Therefore, rather than lead him in a prayer of repentance, it is wise to encourage him to pray himself.

When Nathan confronted David about his sin, he didn't lead the king in a prayer of repentance. If a man committed adultery, and his wife is willing to take him back, should you have to write out an apology for him to read to her? No. Sorrow for his betrayal of her trust should spill from his lips. She doesn't want eloquent words, but simply sorrow of heart. The same applies to a prayer of repentance. The words aren't as important as the presence of "godly sorrow." The sinner should be told to repent—to confess and forsake his sins. He could do this as a whispered prayer, then you could pray for him. If he's not sure what to say, perhaps David's prayer of repentance (Psalm 51) could be used as a model, but his own words are more desirable.

6   There was a man sent from God, whose name was John.

7   The same came for a witness, to bear witness of the Light, that all men through him might believe.

8   He was not that Light, but was sent to bear witness of that Light.

9   That was the true Light, which lights every man that comes into the world.

10 He was in the world, and the world was made by him, and the world knew him not.

11 He came to his own, and his own received him not.

12 But as many as received him, to them gave he power to become the sons of God, even to them that believe on his name:

13 Which were born, not of blood, nor of the will of the flesh, nor of the will of man, but of God.

14 And the Word was made flesh, and dwelt among us, (and we beheld his glory, the glory as of the only begotten of the Father,) full of grace and truth.

15 John bare witness of him, and cried, saying, This was he of whom I spoke, He that comes after me is preferred before me: for he was before me.

16 And of his fulness have all we received, and grace for grace.

17 For the law was given by Moses, but grace and truth came by Jesus Christ.

18 No man has seen God at any time; the only begotten Son, which is in the bosom of the Father, he has declared him.

19 And this is the record of John, when the Jews sent priests and Levites from Jerusalem to ask him, Who are you?

20 And he confessed, and denied not; but confessed, I am not the Christ.

21 And they asked him, What then? are you Elijah? And he said, I am not. Are you that prophet? And he answered, No.

1:13 How to get false converts. Our aim should be to ensure that sinners are born of the Spirit—of the will of God and not of the will of man. Too many of our "decisions" are not a work of the Spirit, but a work of our sincere but manipulative practices. It is simple to secure a decision for Jesus by using this popular method: "Do you know whether you are going to heaven when you die? God wants you to have that assurance. All you need to do is: 1) realize that you are a sinner ('All have sinned, and come short of the glory of God'), and 2) believe that Jesus died on the cross for you. Would you like me to pray with you right now so that you can give your heart to Jesus? Then you will have the assurance that you are going to heaven when you die." For the biblical way to present the gospel, see John 4:7–26 comment.

1:17 "A wrong understanding of the harmony between Law and grace would produce 'error on the left and the right hand.'" John Newton

Questions & Objections

1:18 *"I will believe if God will appear to me."*

A proud and ignorant sinner who says this has no understanding of the nature of His Creator. No man has ever seen the essence of God. (When God "appeared" to certain men in the Old Testament, He manifested Himself in other forms, such as a burning bush or "the Angel of the Lord.") When Moses asked to see God's glory, God told him, "I will make all my goodness pass before you,...[but] you cannot see my face: for there shall no man see me, and live" (Exodus 33:18–23). If all of God's "goodness" were shown to a sinner, he would instantly die. God's "goodness" would just spill wrath upon evil man.

However, the Lord told Moses, "It shall come to pass, while my glory passes by, that I will put you in a cleft of the rock, and will cover you with My hand while I pass by." The only way a sinner can live in the presence of a holy God is to be hidden in the Rock of Jesus Christ (1 Corinthians 10:4).

22   Then said they to him, Who are you? that we may give an answer to them that sent us. What do you say of yourself?
23   He said, I am the voice of one crying in the wilderness, Make straight the way of the Lord, as said the prophet Isaiah.
24   And they which were sent were of the Pharisees.
25   And they asked him, and said to him, Why do you baptize then, if you be not that Christ, nor Elijah, neither that prophet?
26   John answered them, saying, I baptize with water: but there stands one among you, whom you know not;
27   He it is, who coming after me is preferred before me, whose shoe's latchet I am not worthy to unloose.
28   These things were done in Bethabara beyond Jordan, where John was baptizing.
29   The next day John saw Jesus coming to him, and said, Behold the Lamb of God, which takes away the sin of the world.
30   This is he of whom I said, After me comes a man which is preferred before me: for he was before me.

1:32   Messianic prophecy fulfilled: "And the spirit of the Lord shall rest upon him, the spirit of wisdom and understanding, the spirit of counsel and might, the spirit of knowledge and of the fear of the Lord" (Isaiah 11:2). See John 6:14 comment.

31 And I knew him not: but that he should be made manifest to Israel, therefore am I come baptizing with water.

32 And John bare record, saying, I saw the Spirit descending from heaven like a dove, and it abode upon him.

33 And I knew him not: but he that sent me to baptize with water, the same said to me, Upon whom you shall see the Spirit descending, and remaining on him, the same is he which baptizes with the Holy Spirit.

34 And I saw, and bare record that this is the Son of God.

35 Again the next day after John stood, and two of his disciples;

36 And looking upon Jesus as he walked, he said, Behold the Lamb of God!

37 And the two disciples heard him speak, and they followed Jesus.

38 Then Jesus turned, and saw them following, and said to them, What do you seek? They said to him, Rabbi, (which is to say, being interpreted, Master,) where do you dwell?

39 He said to them, Come and see. They came and saw where he dwelt, and abode with him that day: for it was about the tenth hour.

40 One of the two which heard John speak, and followed him, was Andrew, Simon Peter's brother.

"I believe that lack of efficient personal work is one of the failures of the Church today. The people of the Church are like squirrels in a cage. Lots of activity, but accomplishing nothing. It doesn't require a Christian life to sell oyster soup or run a bazaar or a rummage sale..."

Billy Sunday

1:41 After we have found the Messiah, we are to tell others about Him. The only "failure" when it comes to reaching out to the lost is not to be doing it. "Many churches report no new members on confession of faith. Why these meager results with this tremendous expenditure of energy and money? Why are so few people coming into the Kingdom? I will tell you—there is not a definite effort put forth to persuade a definite person to receive a definite Savior at a definite time, and that definite time is now." Billy Sunday

"Our forefathers must be asking, 'How is it that we did so much with so little, and you do so little with so much?'" R. Albert Mohler Jr.

41 He first found his own brother Simon, and said to him, We have found the Messiah, which is, being interpreted, the Christ.

42 And he brought him to Jesus. And when Jesus beheld him, he said, You are Simon the son of Jonah: you shall be called Cephas, which is by interpretation, A stone.

43 The day following Jesus went forth into Galilee, and found Philip, and said to him, Follow me.

44 Now Philip was of Bethsaida, the city of Andrew and Peter.

45 Philip found Nathanael, and said to him, We have found him, of whom Moses in the law, and the prophets, did write, Jesus of Nazareth, the son of Joseph.

46 And Nathanael said to him, Can there any good thing come out of Nazareth? Philip said to him, Come and see.

47 Jesus saw Nathanael coming to him, and said of him, Behold an Israelite indeed, in whom is no guile!

48 Nathanael said to him, Where do you know me from? Jesus answered and said to him, Before that Philip called you, when you were under the fig tree, I saw you.

49 Nathanael answered and said to him, Rabbi, you are the Son of God; you are the King of Israel.

50 Jesus answered and said to him, Because I said to you, I saw you under the fig tree, do you believe? you shall see greater things than these.

1:46 Come and see. Jesus called Philip to follow Him, then Philip immediately found Nathanael and told him about the Savior. Nathanael's question is a typical reaction of the contemporary world to those who follow the Savior. To the cynical, Christians are intellectual wimps, prudes, rejects—unlearned cripples who need some sort of crutch to get them through life. So it is understandable for them to ask, "Can any good thing come out of Christianity?" Down through the ages, its good name has been tainted with the stained brush of hypocrisy, dead religion, and more recently, fanatical sects and televangelism.

Philip merely answered Nathanael's cynicism with the same thing Jesus said to Andrew—"Come and see." Skeptic, come and see. Atheist, come and see. Intellectual, come and see. Just come with a humble and teachable heart, and you who are sightless will see and know that this Man from Nazareth is the Son of God.

1:47 Nathanael was "an Israelite indeed, in whom is no guile." He was a Jew in deed, not just in word. As an honest Jew he didn't twist the Law, as did the Pharisees. He read it in truth. The Law and the prophets had pointed him to Jesus and he was therefore ready to come to the Savior.

51   And he said to him, Verily, verily, I say to you, Hereafter you shall see heaven open, and the angels of God ascending and descending upon the Son of man.

Chapter 2

And the third day there was a marriage in Cana of Galilee; and the mother of Jesus was there:

2   And both Jesus was called, and his disciples, to the marriage.

3   And when they wanted wine, the mother of Jesus said to him, They have no wine.

4   Jesus said to her, Woman, what have I to do with you? mine hour is not yet come.

5   His mother said to the servants, Whatsoever he says to you, do it.

6   And there were set there six waterpots of stone, after the manner of the purifying of the Jews, containing two or three firkins apiece.

7   Jesus said to them, Fill the waterpots with water. And they filled them up to the brim.

8   And he said to them, Draw out now, and bear to the governor of the feast. And they bare it.

9   When the ruler of the feast had tasted the water that was made wine, and knew not whence it was: (but the servants which drew the water knew;) the governor of the feast called the bridegroom,

10   And said to him, Every man at the beginning does set forth good wine; and when men have well drunk, then that which is worse: but you have kept the good wine until now.

11   This beginning of miracles did Jesus in Cana of Galilee, and manifested forth his glory; and his disciples believed on him.

12   After this he went down to Capernaum, he, and his mother, and his brethren, and his disciples: and they continued there not many days.

13   And the Jews' passover was at hand, and Jesus went up to Jerusalem,

14   And found in the temple those that sold oxen and sheep and doves, and the changers of money sitting:

15   And when he had made a scourge of small cords, he drove them all out of the temple, and the sheep, and the oxen; and poured out the changers' money, and overthrew the tables;

16   And said to them that sold doves, Take these things hence; make not my Father's house an house of merchandise.

17   And his disciples remembered that it was written, The zeal of your house has eaten me up.

18   Then answered the Jews and said to him, What sign do you show to us, seeing that you do these things?

2:6-11 *The Significance of the First Miracle*

1. The turning of water into blood was the first of the public miracles that Moses did in Egypt (Exodus 7:20), and the water into wine was the first of the public miracles that Jesus did in the world (John 2:11).

2. The signs that God gave to Egypt in the Old Testament were plagues, destruction, and death, and the signs that Jesus did in the world in the New Testament were healings, blessings, and life.

3. The turning of water to blood initiated Moses (a type of the Savior—Deuteronomy 18:15) leading his people out of the bondage of Egypt into an earthly liberty; the turning of water into wine initiated Jesus taking His people out of the bondage of the corruption of the world into the glorious liberty of the children of God (Romans 8:21).

4. The turning of water to blood culminated in the firstborn in Egypt being delivered to death, while turning the water into wine culminated in the life of the Firstborn being delivered from death (Colossians 1:18).

5. The Law was a ministration of death, the gospel a ministration of life. One was written on cold tablets of stone, the other on the warm fleshly tablets of the heart. One was a ministration of sin unto condemnation and bondage, the other a ministration of righteousness unto life and liberty (2 Corinthians 3:7–9).

6. When Moses changed the water into blood, we are told that all the fish in the river died. When Jesus initiated the new covenant, the catch of the fish are made alive in the net of the kingdom of God (Matthew 4:19).

7. The river of blood was symbolic of death for Egypt, but the water into wine is symbolic of life for the world. The letter of the Law kills, but the Spirit makes alive (2 Corinthians 3:6).

8. When Moses turned the waters of Egypt into blood, the river reeked and made the Egyptians search for another source of water supply (Exodus 7:21,24). When the Law of Moses does its work in the sinner, it makes life odious for him. The weight of sin on his back becomes unbearable as he begins to labor and be heavy laden under its weight. Like the Egyptians, he begins to search for another spring of water; he begins to "thirst for righteousness," because he knows that without a right standing with God, he will perish.

9. Moses turned water into blood, and Jesus' blood turned into water (1 John 5:6). They both poured from His side (John 19:34), perhaps signifying that both Law and grace found harmony in the Savior's death—"Mercy and truth are met together; righteousness and peace have kissed each other" (Psalm 85:10).

10. The water of the old covenant ran out. It could do nothing but leave the sinner with a thirst for righteousness. But as with the wine at Cana, God saved the best until last. The new wine given on the Day of Pentecost (Acts 2:13; Ephesians 5:18) was the Bridegroom giving us the new and "better" covenant (Hebrews 8:5,6).

19 Jesus answered and said to them, Destroy this temple, and in three days I will raise it up.

20 Then said the Jews, Forty and six years was this temple in building, and will you rear it up in three days?

21 But he spoke of the temple of his body.

22 When therefore he was risen from the dead, his disciples remembered that he had said this to them; and they believed the scripture, and the word which Jesus had said.

23 Now when he was in Jerusalem at the passover, in the feast day, many believed in his name, when they saw the miracles which he did.

24 But Jesus did not commit himself to them, because he knew all men,

25 And needed not that any should testify of man: for he knew what was in man.

2:13–17   Cleansing the temple. When Jesus went to the temple, He found it to be filled with those buying and selling merchandise. According to the Jewish historian Josephus, at each Passover, over 250,000 animals were sacrificed. The priests sold licenses to the dealers and therefore would have had a great source of income from the Passover. When the Bible called them "changers of money," it was an appropriate term.

There is, however, another theft going on in another temple. Mankind was made as a dwelling place for his Creator. God made him a little lower than the angels, crowned him with glory and honor, and set him over the works of His hands (Hebrews 2:7), yet sin has given the dwelling place to the devil. The thief, who came to steal, kill, and destroy, is making merchandise out of mankind. Instead of the heart of man being a temple of the Living God (2 Corinthians **6:16)**—a house of prayer—iniquity has made it a den of thieves.

When someone repents and calls upon the name of Jesus Christ, He turns the tables on the devil. The ten stinging cords of the Ten Commandments in the hand of the Savior cleanse the temple of sin. Charles Spurgeon had a resolute grasp of the Law. In preaching to sinners, he said, "I would that this whip would fall upon your backs, that you might be flogged out of your self-righteousness and made to fly to Jesus Christ and find shelter there."

2:15 This is the Lord's righteous indignation at Israel's equivalent of money-hungry televangelists.

2:24,25 "We may deceive all the people sometimes; we may deceive some of the people all the time, but not all the people all the time, and not God at any time." Abraham Lincoln
"Character is what you are in the dark." D. L. Moody

Questions & Objections

3:3 *"I have been born again many times."*

Like Nicodemus, many people have no concept of what it means to be born again. He thought Jesus was speaking of a physical rebirth. Others see the experience as being a spiritual "tingle" when they think of God or a warm fuzzy feeling when they enter a building they erroneously call a "Church." Or maybe they are of the impression that one is born again when one is "christened" or "confirmed." However, the new birth spoken of by Jesus is absolutely essential for sinners to enter heaven. If they are not born again, they will not enter the kingdom of God. Therefore it is necessary to establish the fact that one becomes a Christian by being born again, pointing out that Jesus Himself said that the experience was crucial. The difference between believing in Jesus and being born again is like believing in a parachute, and putting one on. The difference will be seen when you jump. (See Romans 13:14.)

How is one born again? Simply through repentance toward God and faith in the Lord Jesus Christ. Confess and forsake your sins, and trust in Jesus alone for your eternal salvation. When you do, you receive spiritual life through the Holy Spirit who comes to live within you.

Chapter 3

There was a man of the Pharisees, named Nicodemus, a ruler of the Jews:

2   The same came to Jesus by night, and said to him, Rabbi, we know that you are a teacher come from God: for no man can do these miracles that you do, except God be with him.

3   Jesus answered and said to him, Verily, verily, I say to you, Except a man be born again, he cannot see the kingdom of God.

4   Nicodemus said to him, How can a man be born when he is old? can he enter the second time into his mother's womb, and be born?

5   Jesus answered, Verily, verily, I say to you, Except a man be born of water and of the Spirit, he cannot enter into the kingdom of God.

6   That which is born of the flesh is flesh; and that which is born of the Spirit is spirit.

7   Marvel not that I said to you, You must be born again.

8   The wind blows where it lists, and you hear the sound thereof, but can not tell whence it comes, and where it goes: so is every one that is born of the Spirit.

3:16 *Is Repentance Necessary for Salvation?*

It is true that numerous Bible verses speak of the promise of salvation with no mention of repentance. These verses merely say to "believe" on Jesus Christ and you shall be saved (Acts 16:31; Romans 10:9). However, the Bible makes it clear that God is holy and man is sinful, and that sin makes a separation between the two (Isaiah 59:1,2). Without repentance from sin, wicked men cannot have fellowship with a holy God. We are dead in our trespasses and sins (Ephesians 2:1) and until we forsake them through repentance, we cannot be made alive in Christ. The Scriptures speak of "repentance unto life" (Acts 11:18). We turn from sin to the Savior. This is why Paul preached "repentance toward God, and faith toward our Lord Jesus Christ" (Acts 20:21).

The first public word Jesus preached was "repent" (Matthew 4:17). John the Baptist began his ministry the same way (Matthew 3:2). Jesus told His hearers that without repentance, they would perish (Luke 13:3). If belief is all that is necessary for salvation, then the logical conclusion is that one need never repent. However, the Bible tells us that a false convert "believes" and yet is not saved (Luke 8:13); he remains a "worker of iniquity." Look at the warning of Scripture: "If we say that we have fellowship with him, and walk in darkness, we lie, and do not the truth" (1 John 1:6). The Scriptures also say, "He that covers his sins shall not prosper, but whoso confesses and forsakes them [repentance] shall have mercy" (Proverbs 28:13). Jesus said that there was joy in heaven over one sinner who "repents" (Luke 15:10). If there is no repentance, there is no joy because there is no salvation.

As Peter preached on the Day of Pentecost, he commanded his hearers to repent "for the remission of sins" (Acts 2:38). Without repentance, there is no remission of sins; we are still under God's wrath. Peter further said, "Repent...and be converted, that your sins may be blotted out" (Acts 3:19). We cannot be "converted" unless we repent. God Himself "commands all men everywhere [leaving no exceptions] to repent" (Acts 17:30). Peter said a similar thing at Pentecost: "Repent, and be baptized every one of you" (Acts 2:38).

If repentance wasn't necessary for salvation, why then did Jesus command that repentance be preached to all nations (Luke 24:47)? With so many Scriptures speaking of the necessity of repentance for salvation, one can only suspect that those who preach salvation without repentance are strangers to repentance themselves, and thus strangers to true conversion.

3:2 Grace to the humble. Nicodemus was a humble Jew (he acknowledged the deity of the Son of God), and he knew the Law (he was a "master of Israel," v. 10); therefore, Jesus gave him the good news of the gospel. He was convinced of the disease of sin and consequently ready to hear of the cure.

3:3 "These verses aren't necessarily about what Nicodemus asked Jesus; they are about what Jesus knew. The last verse of the previous chapter said that He knew what was in man. Jesus knew what was in the heart of Nicodemus: he was a Law-breaker, and he needed to be born again." Garry T. Ansdell, D.D.

9   Nicodemus answered and said to him, How can these things be?
10   Jesus answered and said to him, Are you a master of Israel, and know not these things?
11   Verily, verily, I say to you, We speak that we do know, and testify that we have seen; and you receive not our witness.
12   If I have told you earthly things, and you believe not, how shall you believe, if I tell you of heavenly things?
13   And no man has ascended up to heaven, but he that came down from heaven, even the Son of man which is in heaven.
14   And as Moses lifted up the serpent in the wilderness, even so must the Son of man be lifted up:
15   That whosoever believes in him should not perish, but have eternal life.
16   For God so loved the world, that he gave his only begotten Son, that whosoever believes in him should not perish, but have everlasting life.
17   For God sent not his Son into the world to condemn the world; but that the world through him might be saved.
18   He that believes on him is not condemned: but he that believes not is condemned already, because he has not believed in the name of the only begotten Son of God.
19   And this is the condemnation, that light is come into the world, and men loved darkness rather than light, because their deeds were evil.
20   For every one that does evil hates the light, neither comes to the light, lest his deeds should be reproved.
21   But he that does truth comes to the light, that his deeds may be made manifest, that they are wrought in God.
22   After these things came Jesus and his disciples into the land of Judea; and there he tarried with them, and baptized.

3:7 New birth—its necessity for salvation. This is a fulfillment of Ezekiel **36:26**: "A new heart also will I give you, and a new spirit will I put within you: and I will take away the stony heart out of your flesh, and I will give you an heart of flesh." Man cannot enter heaven in his spiritually dead state; he must be born again to have spiritual life. Jesus said that He is life (John 14:6; John 11:25,26), and that we must come to Him to have life (John 5:39,40; 1 John 5:11,12). Those who trust in Christ are "born again, not of corruptible seed, but of incorruptible, by the word of God, which lives and abides for ever" (1 Peter 1:23). See 2 Corinthians 5:17.

"Ever since Adam sinned, the earth has been the land of the walking dead—spiritually dead. What is the disease that killed man? 'The wages of sin is death.' So from God's point of view, salvation involves the raising of spiritually dead men to life. But before God could give life to the dead, He had to totally eradicate the fatal disease that killed men—sin. So the cross was God's method of dealing with the disease called sin, and the resurrection of Christ was and is God's method of giving life to the dead!" Bob George, Classic Christianity

3:14,15 When fiery serpents were sent among Israel, they caused the Israelites to admit that they had sinned. The means of their salvation was to look up to a bronze serpent that Moses had placed on a pole. Those who had been bitten and were doomed to die could look at the bronze serpent and live (Numbers 21:6–9). In John 3:14,15, Jesus specifically cited this Old Testament passage in reference to salvation from sin.

The Ten Commandments are like ten biting serpents that carry with them the venomous curse of the Law. They drive sinners to look to the One lifted up on a cross, and those who look to Him will live. It was the Law of Moses that put Jesus on the cross. The Messiah became a curse for us, and redeemed us from the curse of the Law.

---

23 And John also was baptizing in Aenon near to Salim, because there was much water there: and they came, and were baptized.

24 For John was not yet cast into prison.

25 Then there arose a question between some of John's disciples and the Jews about purifying.

26 And they came to John, and said to him, Rabbi, he that was with you beyond Jordan, to whom you bare witness, behold, the same baptizes, and all men come to him.

27 John answered and said, A man can receive nothing, except it be given him from heaven.

Using the Law in Evangelism

3:16 "If I had my way, I would declare a moratorium on public preaching of 'the plan of salvation' in America for one to two years. Then I would call on everyone who has use of the airwaves and the pulpits to preach the holiness of God, the righteousness of God, and the Law of God, until sinners would cry out, 'What must we do to be saved?' Then I would take them off in a corner and whisper the gospel to them. Don't use John 3:16. Such drastic action is needed because we have gospel-hardened a generation of sinners by telling them how to be saved before they have any understanding why they need to be saved." Paris Reidhead

28   You yourselves bear me witness, that I said, I am not the Christ, but that I am sent before him.

29   He that has the bride is the bridegroom: but the friend of the bridegroom, which stands and hears him, rejoices greatly because of the bridegroom's voice: this my joy therefore is fulfilled.

30   He must increase, but I must decrease.

31   He that comes from above is above all: he that is of the earth is earthly, and speaks of the earth: he that comes from heaven is above all.

32   And what he has seen and heard, that he testifies; and no man receives his testimony.

33 He that has received his testimony has set to his seal that God is true.

34 For he whom God has sent speaks the words of God: for God gives not the Spirit by measure to him.

35 The Father loves the Son, and has given all things into his hand.

36 He that believes on the Son has everlasting life: and he that believes not the Son shall not see life; but the wrath of God abides on him.

66 Sin and hell are married unless repentance proclaims the divorce. 99
Charles Spurgeon

Chapter 4

When therefore the Lord knew how the Pharisees had heard that Jesus made and baptized more disciples than John,

2   (Though Jesus himself baptized not, but his disciples,)

3   He left Judea, and departed again into Galilee.

4   And he must needs go through Samaria.

3:16,17 Salvation is possible for every person. See John 4:14.

3:16,17 God Himself provided our way of escape: "But God commends his love toward us, in that, while we were yet sinners, Christ died for us" (Romans 5:8). "For he has made him to be sin for us, who knew no sin; that we might be made the righteousness of God in him" (2 Corinthians 5:21). "But he was wounded for our transgressions, he was bruised for our iniquities: the chastisement of our peace was upon him; and with his stripes we are healed. All we like sheep have gone astray; we have turned every one to his own way; and the Lord has laid on him the iniquity of us all" (Isaiah 53:5,6). See Romans 10:9 comment.

3:19 Jesus said that we loved the darkness of sin rather than the light of righteousness, because the human heart finds pleasure in sin. If you don't believe it, visit the "adult" section of your local video store. Look at the covers to see the type of entertainment the hearts of men and women crave—unspeakable violence, inconceivable horror, and unending sexual perversion.

3:19,20 The same sunlight that melts wax also hardens clay. As God's light shines on man, the sinner's heart determines his response. One whose heart is tender will respond to God; one whose heart is bent on evil will harden his heart further against God and will remain in darkness. Sinners should note: After Pharaoh repeatedly hardened his heart against God (Exodus 8:15,32), God then hardened Pharaoh's heart (Exodus 10:27). Those who continually reject God will be given up to "uncleanness, vile affections, and a reprobate mind" (Romans 1:24,26,28).

---

5   Then came he to a city of Samaria, which is called Sychar, near to the parcel of ground that Jacob gave to his son Joseph.

6   Now Jacob's well was there. Jesus therefore, being wearied with his journey, sat thus on the well: and it was about the sixth hour.

7   There came a woman of Samaria to draw water: Jesus said to her, Give me to drink.

8   (For his disciples were gone away to the city to buy meat.)

9   Then said the woman of Samaria to him, How is it that you, being a Jew, ask drink of me, which am a woman of Samaria? for the Jews have no dealings with the Samaritans.

10   Jesus answered and said to her, If you knew the gift of God, and who it is that said to you, Give me to drink; you would have asked of him, and he would have given you living water.

11   The woman said to him, Sir, you have nothing to draw with, and the well is deep: from whence then have you that living water?

4:7 *Personal Witnessing—How Jesus Did It*

How to address the sinner's conscience and speak with someone who doesn't believe in hell

Verses 7–26 give us the Master's example of how to share our faith. Notice that Jesus spoke to the woman at the well when she was alone. We will often find that people are more open and honest when they are alone. So, if possible, pick a person who is sitting by himself. From these verses, we can see four clear principles to follow.

First: Jesus began in the natural realm (v. 7). This woman was unregenerate, and the Bible tells us "the natural man receives not the things of the Spirit of God" (1 Corinthians 2:14). He therefore spoke of something she could relate to—water. Most of us can strike up a conversation with a stranger in the natural realm. It may be a friendly "How are you doing?" or a warm "Good morning!" If the person responds with a sense of warmth, we may then ask, "Do you live around here?" and from there develop a conversation.

Second: Jesus swung the conversation to the spiritual realm (v. 10). He simply mentioned the things of God. This will take courage. We may say something like, "Did you go to church on Sunday?" or "Did you see that Christian TV program last week?" If the person responds positively, the question "Do you have a Christian background?" will probe his background. He may answer, "I went to church when I was a child, but I drifted away from it."

Another simple way to swing to the spiritual is to offer the person a gospel tract and ask, "Did you get one of these?" When he takes it, simply say, "It's a gospel tract. Do you come from a Christian background?"

Third: Jesus brought conviction using the Law of God (vv. 16–18). Jesus gently spoke to her conscience by alluding to the fact that she had transgressed the Seventh of the Ten Commandments. He used the Law to bring "the knowledge of sin" (see Romans 3:19,20). We can do the same by asking, "Do you think that you have kept the Ten Commandments?" Most people think they have, so quickly follow with, "Have you ever told a lie?" This is confrontational, but if it's asked in a spirit of love and gentleness, there won't be any offense. Remember that the "work of the Law [is] written in their hearts" and that the conscience will bear "witness" (Romans 2:15). Jesus confronted the rich young ruler in Luke 18:18–21 with five of the Ten Commandments and there was no offense. Have confidence that the conscience will do its work and affirm the truth of each Commandment. Don't be afraid to gently ask, "Have you ever stolen something, even if it's small?" Learn how to open up the spirituality of the Law and show how God considers lust to be the same as adultery (Matthew 5:27,28) and hatred the same as murder (1 John 3:15). Make sure you get an admission of guilt.

Ask the person, "If God judges you by the Ten Commandments on Judgment Day, do you think you will be innocent or guilty?" If he says he will be innocent, ask, "Why is that?" If he admits his guilt, ask, "Do you think you will go to heaven or hell?"

From there the conversation may go one of three ways:

1. He may confidently say, "I don't believe in hell." Gently respond, "That doesn't matter. You still have to face God on Judgment Day whether you believe in it or not. If I step onto the freeway when a massive truck is heading for me and I say, 'I don't believe in trucks,' my lack of belief isn't going to change reality."

Then tenderly tell him he has already admitted to you that he has lied, stolen, and committed adultery in his heart, and that God gave him a conscience so that he would know right from wrong. His conscience and the conviction of the Holy Spirit will do the rest.

That's why it is essential to draw out an admission of guilt before you mention Judgment Day or the existence of hell.

2. He may say that he's guilty, but that he will go to heaven. This is usually because he thinks that God is "good," and that He will, therefore, overlook sin in his case. Point out that if a judge in a criminal case has a guilty murderer standing before him, the judge, if he is a good man, can't just let him go. He must ensure that the guilty man is punished. If God is good, He must (by nature) punish murderers, rapists, thieves, liars, adulterers, fornicators, and those who have lived in rebellion to the inner light that God has given to every man.

3. He may admit that he is guilty and therefore going to hell. Ask him if that concerns him. Speak to him about how much he values his eyes and how much more therefore he should value the salvation of his soul. (For the biblical description of hell, see Revelation 1:18 comment.) If possible, take the person through the linked verses in this Bible, beginning at the Matthew 5:21,22 comment.

(continued on next page)

4:7 continued)

Fourth: Jesus revealed Himself to her (v. 26). Once the Law has humbled the person, he is ready for grace. Remember, the Bible says that God resists the proud and gives grace to the humble (James 4:6). The gospel is for the humble (see Luke 4:18 comment). Only the sick need a physician, and only those who will admit that they have the disease of sin will truly embrace the cure of the gospel.

Learn how to present the work of the cross—that God sent His Son to suffer and die in our place. Tell the sinner of the love of God in Christ; that Jesus rose from the dead and defeated death. Take him back to civil law and say, "It's as simple as this: We broke God's Law, and Jesus paid our fine. If you will repent and trust in the Savior, God will forgive your sins and dismiss your case." Ask him if he understands what you have told him. If he is willing to confess and forsake his sins, and trust the Savior with his eternal salvation, have him pray and ask God to forgive him. Then pray for him. Get him a Bible. Instruct him to read it daily and obey what he reads, and encourage him to get into a Bible-believing, Christ-preaching church.

12 Are you greater than our father Jacob, which gave us the well, and drank thereof himself, and his children, and his cattle?

13 Jesus answered and said to her, Whosoever drinks of this water shall thirst again:

14 But whosoever drinks of the water that I shall give him shall never thirst; but the water that I shall give him shall be in him a well of water springing up into everlasting life.

15 The woman said to him, Sir, give me this water, that I thirst not, neither come here to draw.

16 Jesus said to her, Go, call your husband, and come here.

17 The woman answered and said, I have no husband. Jesus said to her, You have well said, I have no husband:

18 For you have had five husbands; and he whom you now have is not your husband: in that you said truly.

19 The woman said to him, Sir, I perceive that you are a prophet.

20 Our fathers worshipped in this mountain; and you say, that in Jerusalem is the place where men ought to worship.

21 Jesus said to her, Woman, believe me, the hour comes, when you shall neither in this mountain, nor yet at Jerusalem, worship the Father.

22 You worship you know not what: we know what we worship: for salvation is of the Jews.

23 But the hour comes, and now is, when the true worshippers shall worship the Father in spirit and in truth: for the Father seeks such to worship him.

24 God is a Spirit: and they that worship him must worship him in spirit and in truth.

25 The woman said to him, I know that Messiah comes, which is called Christ: when he is come, he will tell us all things.

26 Jesus said to her, I that speak to you am he.

27 And upon this came his disciples, and marveled that he talked with the woman: yet no man said, What do you seek? or, Why do you talk with her?

28 The woman then left her waterpot, and went her way into the city, and said to the men,

29 Come, see a man, which told me all things that ever I did: is not this the Christ?

30 Then they went out of the city, and came to him.

> When your will is God's will, you will have your will.
> Charles Spurgeon

31 In the mean while his disciples prayed him, saying, Master, eat.

32 But he said to them, I have meat to eat that you know not of.

33 Therefore said the disciples one to another, has any man brought him anything to eat?

34 Jesus said to them, My meat is to do the will of him that sent me, and to finish his work.

35 Do you not say, There are yet four months, and then comes harvest? behold, I say to you, Lift up your eyes, and look on the fields; for they are white already to harvest.

36 And he that reaps receives wages, and gathers fruit to life eternal: that both he that sows and he that reaps may rejoice together.

37 And herein is that saying true, One sows, and another reaps.

38 I sent you to reap that whereon you bestowed no labour: other men laboured, and you are entered into their labours.

39 And many of the Samaritans of that city believed on him for the saying of the woman, which testified, He told me all that ever I did.

40 So when the Samaritans were come to him, they besought him that he would tarry with them: and he abode there two days.

4:14 Salvation is possible for every person. See John 6:51.

4:34 The "meat" that nourished the Savior was to carry out the work of evangelism—to seek and to save that which was lost.

41 And many more believed because of his own word;

42 And said to the woman, Now we believe, not because of your saying: for we have heard him ourselves, and know that this is indeed the Christ, the Savior of the world.

43 Now after two days he departed thence, and went into Galilee.

44 For Jesus himself testified, that a prophet has no honor in his own country.

45 Then when he was come into Galilee, the Galilaeans received him, having seen all the things that he did at Jerusalem at the feast: for they also went to the feast.

46 So Jesus came again into Cana of Galilee, where he made the water wine. And there was a certain nobleman, whose son was sick at Capernaum.

47 When he heard that Jesus was come out of Judea into Galilee, he went to him, and besought him that he would come down, and heal his son: for he was at the point of death.

48 Then said Jesus to him, Except you see signs and wonders, you will not believe.

49 The nobleman said to him, Sir, come down ere my child die.

50 Jesus said to him, Go your way; your son lives. And the man believed the word that Jesus had spoken to him, and he went his way.

51 And as he was now going down, his servants met him, and told him, saying, Your son lives.

52 Then inquired he of them the hour when he began to amend. And they said to him, Yesterday at the seventh hour the fever left him.

4:36 "I would think it a greater happiness to gain one soul to Christ than mountains of silver and gold to myself." Matthew Henry

4:37,38 **The measure of success.** Don't be tempted to measure evangelistic "success" by the number of "decisions" obtained. We tend to rejoice over decisions, when heaven reserves its rejoicing for repentance—"There is joy in the presence of the angels of God over one sinner that repents" (Luke 15:10). It is easy to get "decisions for Jesus" using the modern method of well-chosen words and psychological manipulation. Rather, see success as having the opportunity to sow the seed of God's Word into the hearts of your hearers. If you faithfully sow, someone else will reap. If you have the privilege of reaping, then someone has faithfully sown before you. One sows, another reaps, but it is God who gives the increase. See 1 Corinthians 3:6,7.

53 So the father knew that it was at the same hour, in the which Jesus said to him, Your son lives: and himself believed, and his whole house.
54 This is again the second miracle that Jesus did, when he was come out of Judea into Galilee.

Chapter 5

After this there was a feast of the Jews; and Jesus went up to Jerusalem.
2 Now there is at Jerusalem by the sheep market a pool, which is called in the Hebrew tongue Bethesda, having five porches.
3 In these lay a great multitude of impotent folk, of blind, halt, withered, waiting for the moving of the water.
4 For an angel went down at a certain season into the pool, and troubled the water: whosoever then first after the troubling of the water stepped in was made whole of whatsoever disease he had.
5 And a certain man was there, which had an infirmity thirty and eight years.
6 When Jesus saw him lie, and knew that he had been now a long time in that case, he said to him, Will you be made whole?
7 The impotent man answered him, Sir, I have no man, when the water is troubled, to put me into the pool: but while I am coming, another steps down before me.
8 Jesus said to him, Rise, take up your bed, and walk.
9 And immediately the man was made whole, and took up his bed, and walked: and on the same day was the sabbath.
10 The Jews therefore said to him that was cured, It is the sabbath day: it is not lawful for you to carry your bed.
11 He answered them, He that made me whole, the same said to me, Take up your bed, and walk.

5:14 We once lay as feeble, fragile, and frail folk, helpless and hopeless, pathetically paralyzed by the devil—"taken captive to do his will" until Jesus spoke a word to us. We were on a deathbed of sin with no one able to help us, but we heard the voice of the Word of God saying: "Arise from the dead, and Christ shall give you light" (Ephesians 5:14).

Now a thankful heart for the unspeakable gift makes us want to be always in the presence of God. Unlike the healed man, however, we need not go to the temple to thank the Father, for He now abides in the heart of the believer. The work of Calvary has made the believer the temple of the Living God. See 2 Corinthians 6:16.

12 Then asked they him, What man is that which said to you, Take up your bed, and walk?

13 And he that was healed did not know who it was: for Jesus had conveyed himself away, a multitude being in that place.

14 Afterward Jesus found him in the temple, and said to him, Behold, you are made whole: sin no more, lest a worse thing come to you.

15 The man departed, and told the Jews that it was Jesus, which had made him whole.

16 And therefore did the Jews persecute Jesus, and sought to slay him, because he had done these things on the sabbath day.

17 But Jesus answered them, My Father works hitherto, and I work.

18 Therefore the Jews sought the more to kill him, because he not only had broken the sabbath, but said also that God was his Father, making himself equal with God.

19 Then answered Jesus and said to them, Verily, verily, I say to you, The Son can do nothing of himself, but what he sees the Father do: for what things soever he does, these also does the Son likewise.

20 For the Father loves the Son, and shows him all things that himself does: and he will show him greater works than these, that you may marvel.

21 For as the Father raises up the dead, and quickens them; even so the Son quickens whom he will.

5:17 Jesus' claims. Jesus was either God in human form, or a crackpot. There is no middle ground. In verses 17–29 He said:

• Whatever He saw the Father do, He did.

• God showed Jesus everything He did and He had even greater things to show Him, which would cause the people to be astonished.

• Just as God raised the dead and gave life to them, so Jesus gives life to whomever He would.

• God Himself had appointed Jesus of Nazareth as the Judge of all mankind.

• Humanity should honor Jesus as much as they honor the Father.

• Those who didn't honor Jesus didn't honor God.

• All who heard His words and trusted in the Father escape the wrath of the Law.

• All who trusted Him passed from death to life.

• The hour would come when everyone in their graves would hear the voice of Jesus and be raised from the dead.

• As God is the source of all life, so He has given Jesus life in Himself.

22 For the Father judges no man, but has committed all judgment to the Son:

23 That all men should honor the Son, even as they honor the Father. He that honors not the Son honors not the Father which has sent him.

24 Verily, verily, I say to you, He that hears my word, and believes on him that sent me, has everlasting life, and shall not come into condemnation; but is passed from death to life.

25 Verily, verily, I say to you, The hour is coming, and now is, when the dead shall hear the voice of the Son of God: and they that hear shall live.

26 For as the Father has life in himself; so has he given to the Son to have life in himself;

27 And has given him authority to execute judgment also, because he is the Son of man.

Halloween can be an incredible opportunity for sharing the Gospel. See 1 Timothy 4:1 comment.

28 Marvel not at this: for the hour is coming, in the which all that are in the graves shall hear his voice,

29 And shall come forth; they that have done good, to the resurrection of life; and they that have done evil, to the resurrection of damnation.

30 I can of mine own self do nothing: as I hear, I judge: and my judgment is just; because I seek not mine own will, but the will of the Father which has sent me.

31 If I bear witness of myself, my witness is not true.

32 There is another that bears witness of me; and I know that the witness which he witnesses of me is true.

33 You sent to John, and he bare witness to the truth.

34 But I receive not testimony from man: but these things I say, that you might be saved.

35 He was a burning and a shining light: and you were willing for a season to rejoice in his light.

36 But I have greater witness than that of John: for the works which the Father has given me to finish, the same works that I do, bear witness of me, that the Father has sent me.

37 And the Father himself, which has sent me, has borne witness of me. You have neither heard his voice at any time, nor seen his shape.

38 And you have not his word abiding
in you: for whom he has sent, him you
believe not.

39 Search the scriptures; for in them you think you have eternal life:
and they are they which testify of me.

40 And you will not come to me, that you might have life.

41 I receive not honor from men.

42 But I know you, that you have not the love of God in you.

43 I am come in my Father's name, and you receive me not: if another
shall come in his own name, him you will receive.

44 How can you believe, which receive honor one of another, and
seek not the honor that comes from God only?

45 Do not think that I will accuse you to the Father: there is one
that accuses you, even Moses, in whom you trust.

46 For had you believed Moses, you would have believed me: for
he wrote of me.

47 But if you believe not his writings, how shall you believe
my words?

Chapter 6

After these things Jesus went over the sea of Galilee, which is the
sea of Tiberias.

2 And a great multitude followed him, because they saw his miracles
which he did on them that were diseased.

3 And Jesus went up into a mountain, and there he sat with his
disciples.

4 And the passover, a feast of the Jews, was nigh.

5 When Jesus then lifted up his eyes, and saw a great company come to
him, he said to Philip, Whence shall we buy bread, that these may eat?

6 And this he said to prove him: for he himself knew what he
would do.

5:28 Jesus' unique words: Jesus is saying that His voice will raise billions
who have died. Psalm 29:3–9 describes the powerful voice of God. See John
6:38 comment.

5:28,29 Judgment Day: For verses that warn of its reality, see Acts 17:31.

5:39,40 To see why sinners need to come to Jesus to have life, see John 3:7
comment and Ephesians 4:18 "Questions & Objections."

7   Philip answered him, Two hundred pennyworth of bread is not sufficient for them, that every one of them may take a little.

8   One of his disciples, Andrew, Simon Peter's brother, said to him,

9   There is a lad here, which has five barley loaves, and two small fishes: but what are they among so many?

10   And Jesus said, Make the men sit down. Now there was much grass in the place. So the men sat down, in number about five thousand.

11   And Jesus took the loaves; and when he had given thanks, he distributed to the disciples, and the disciples to them that were set down; and likewise of the fishes as much as they would.

12   When they were filled, he said to his disciples, Gather up the fragments that remain, that nothing be lost.

13   Therefore they gathered them together, and filled twelve baskets with the fragments of the five barley loaves, which remained over and above to them that had eaten.

14   Then those men, when they had seen the miracle that Jesus did, said, This is of a truth that prophet that should come into the world.

15   When Jesus therefore perceived that they would come and take him by force, to make him a king, he departed again into a mountain himself alone.

16   And when even was now come, his disciples went down to the sea,

17   And entered into a ship, and went over the sea toward Capernaum. And it was now dark, and Jesus was not come to them.

18   And the sea arose by reason of a great wind that blew.

19   So when they had rowed about five and twenty or thirty furlongs, they see Jesus walking on the sea, and drawing near to the ship: and they were afraid.

20   But he said to them, It is I; be not afraid.

21   Then they willingly received him into the ship: and immediately the ship was at the land where they went.

22   The day following, when the people which stood on the other side of the sea saw that there was none other boat there, save that one whereinto his disciples were entered, and that Jesus went not with his disciples into the boat, but that his disciples were gone away alone;

23   (Howbeit there came other boats from Tiberias near to the place where they did eat bread, after that the Lord had given thanks:)

6:14 Messianic prophecy fulfilled: "The Lord your God will raise up to you a Prophet from your midst, of your brethren, like unto me; to him you shall hearken" (Deuteronomy 18:15). See John 19:29 comment.

24 When the people therefore saw that Jesus was not there, neither his disciples, they also took shipping, and came to Capernaum, seeking for Jesus.

25 And when they had found him on the other side of the sea, they said to him, Rabbi, when did you come here?

26 Jesus answered them and said, Verily, verily, I say to you, You seek me, not because you saw the miracles, but because you did eat of the loaves, and were filled.

27 Labour not for the meat which perishes, but for that meat which endures to everlasting life, which the Son of man shall give to you: for him has God the Father sealed.

28 Then said they to him, What shall we do, that we might work the works of God?

29 Jesus answered and said to them, This is the work of God, that you believe on him whom he has sent.

30 They said therefore to him, What sign do you show then, that we may see, and believe you? what do you work?

31 Our fathers did eat manna in the desert; as it is written, He gave them bread from heaven to eat.

32 Then Jesus said to them, Verily, verily, I say to you, Moses gave you not that bread from heaven; but my Father gives you the true bread from heaven.

33 For the bread of God is he which came down from heaven, and gives life to the world.

34 Then said they to him, Lord, evermore give us this bread.

35 And Jesus said to them, I am the bread of life: he that comes to me shall never hunger; and he that believes on me shall never thirst.

36 But I said to you, That you also have seen me, and believe not.

37 All that the Father gives me shall come to me; and him that comes to me I will in no wise cast out.

38 For I came down from heaven, not to do mine own will, but the will of him that sent me.

6:28,29 Most religions teach that certain works are required in order to be saved. Here God tells us the only "work" He considers: "believe on him whom he has sent."

6:38 Jesus' unique words: Jesus said that He "came down" from heaven, that He was pre-existent. He says elsewhere: "I am from above...I am not of this world" (8:23), and "I proceeded forth and came from God" (8:42). For more on His pre-existence, see John 17:5. See also John 6:47 comment

39 And this is the Father's will which has sent me, that of all which he has given me I should lose nothing, but should raise it up again at the last day.
40 And this is the will of him that sent me, that every one which sees the Son, and believes on him, may have everlasting life: and I will raise him up at the last day.
41 The Jews then murmured at him, because he said, I am the bread which came down from heaven.
42 And they said, Is not this Jesus, the son of Joseph, whose father and mother we know? how is it then that he says, I came down from heaven?
43 Jesus therefore answered and said to them, Murmur not among yourselves.
44 No man can come to me, except the Father which has sent me draw him: and I will raise him up at the last day.

"I know men and I tell you that Jesus Christ is no mere man..." (See what Napoleon had to say about Jesus in John 7:46.)

Napoleon Bonaparte

6:45 Taught by God. "Read and read again, and do not despair of help to understand the will and mind of God though you think they are fast locked up from you. Neither trouble your heads though you have not commentaries and exposition. Pray and read, read and pray; for a little from God is better than a great deal from men. Also, what is from men is uncertain, and is often lost and tumbled over by men; but what is from God is fixed as a nail in a sure place. There is nothing that so abides with us as what we receive from God; and the reason why the Christians in this day are at such a loss as to some things is that they are contented with what comes from men's mouths, without searching and kneeling before God to know of Him the truth of things. Things we receive at God's hands come to us as truths from the minting house, though old in themselves, yet new to us. Old truths are always new to us if they come with the smell of heaven upon them." John Bunyan

6:47 Jesus' unique words: He was saying that He had the authority to grant everlasting life to all who trust in Him. See John 6:53,54 comment.

45 It is written in the prophets, And they shall be all taught of God. Every man therefore that has heard, and has learned of the Father, comes to me.

46 Not that any man has seen the Father, save he which is of God, he has seen the Father.

47 Verily, verily, I say to you, He that believes on me has everlasting life.

48 I am that bread of life.

49 Your fathers did eat manna in the wilderness, and are dead.

50 This is the bread which came down from heaven, that a man may eat thereof, and not die.

51 I am the living bread which came down from heaven: if any man eat of this bread, he shall live for ever: and the bread that I will give is my flesh, which I will give for the life of the world.

52 The Jews therefore strove among themselves, saying, How can this man give us his flesh to eat?

53 Then Jesus said to them, Verily, verily, I say to you, Except you eat the flesh of the Son of man, and drink his blood, you have no life in you.

54 Whoso eats my flesh, and drinks my blood, has eternal life; and I will raise him up at the last day.

55 For my flesh is meat indeed, and my blood is drink indeed.

56 He that eats my flesh, and drinks my blood, dwells in me, and I in him.

57 As the living Father has sent me, and I live by the Father: so he that eats me, even he shall live by me.

58 This is that bread which came down from heaven: not as your fathers did eat manna, and are dead: he that eats of this bread shall live for ever.

59 These things said he in the synagogue, as he taught in Capernaum.

60 Many therefore of his disciples, when they had heard this, said, This is an hard saying; who can hear it?

61 When Jesus knew in himself that his disciples murmured at it, he said to them, Does this offend you?

62 What and if you shall see the Son of man ascend up where he was before?

63 It is the spirit that quickens; the flesh profits nothing: the words that I speak to you, they are spirit, and they are life.

64 But there are some of you that believe not. For Jesus knew from the beginning who they were that believed not, and who should betray him.

65 And he said, Therefore said I to you, that no man can come to me, except it were given to him of my Father.

66 From that time many of his disciples went back, and walked no more with him.

67 Then said Jesus to the twelve, Will you also go away?

68 Then Simon Peter answered him, Lord, to whom shall we go? you have the words of eternal life.

69 And we believe and are sure that you are that Christ, the Son of the living God.

70 Jesus answered them, Have not I chosen you twelve, and one of you is a devil?

71 He spoke of Judas Iscariot the son of Simon: for he it was that should betray him, being one of the twelve.

6:51 Salvation is possible for every person. See John 7:37.

6:53,54 Jesus' unique words: These are the words of a madman...or God in human form. He was not advocating cannibalism, but was speaking in a spiritual sense. Just as we need to eat and drink in order to live, so we must "eat" the Bread of Life (John 6:48,51) and "drink" His "blood, which is shed for you" (Luke 22:20) in order to have spiritual life. Unless we trust in Christ, relying on Him daily for our life-sustaining nourishment, we have no life in us and remain dead in our sins. (See Ephesians 2:1 comment.) See also John 8:51 comment.

6:65 "The impulse to pursue God originates with God." A. W. Tozer

6:68 The uniqueness of Jesus. "This Jesus of Nazareth, without money and arms, conquered more millions than Alexander, Caesar, Mohammed, and Napoleon; without science and learning, He shed more light on things human and divine than all philosophers and scholars combined; without the eloquence of schools, He spoke such words of life as were never spoken before or since, and produced effects which lie beyond the reach of orator or poet; without writing a single line, He set more pens in motion, and furnished themes for more sermons, orations, discussions, learned volumes, works of art, and songs of praise than the whole army of great men of ancient and modern times." Philip Schaff, The Person of Christ

Chapter 7

A fter these things Jesus walked in Galilee: for he would not walk in Jewry, because the Jews sought to kill him.

2   Now the Jews' feast of tabernacles was at hand.

3   His brethren therefore said to him, Depart hence, and go into Judea, that your disciples also may see the works that you do.

4   For there is no man that does any thing in secret, and he himself seeks to be known openly. If you do these things, show yourself to the world.

5   For neither did his brethren believe in him.

6   Then Jesus said to them, My time is not yet come: but your time is always ready.

7   The world cannot hate you; but me it hates, because I testify of it, that the works thereof are evil.

8   Go up to this feast: I go not up yet to this feast; for my time is not yet full come.

9   When he had said these words to them, he abode still in Galilee.

10   But when his brethren were gone up, then went he also up to the feast, not openly, but as it were in secret.

11   Then the Jews sought him at the feast, and said, Where is he?

12   And there was much murmuring among the people concerning him: for some said, He is a good man: others said, Nay; but he deceives the people.

13   Howbeit no man spoke openly of him for fear of the Jews.

14   Now about the midst of the feast Jesus went up into the temple, and taught.

15   And the Jews marveled, saying, How knows this man letters, having never learned?

7:17 In reference to creation, respected Bible teacher Derek Prince said, "I am simple-minded enough to believe that it happened the way the Bible described it. I have been a professor at Britain's largest university [Cambridge] for nine years. I hold various degrees and academic distinctions, and I feel in many ways I am quite sophisticated intellectually, but I don't feel in any way intellectually inferior when I say that I believe the Bible record of creation. Prior to believing the Bible I have studied many other attempts to explain man's origin and found them all unsatisfying and in many cases self-contradictory. I turned to study the Bible as a professional philosopher—not as a believer—and I commented to myself, 'At least it can't be any sillier than some of the other things I've heard,' and to my astonishment, I discovered it had the answer."

The Ten Commandments

You shall have no other gods before Me.

You shall not make to yourself any graven image.

You shall not take the name of the
Lord your God in vain.

Remember the Sabbath day, to keep it holy.

Honor your father and your mother.

You shall not kill.

You shall not commit adultery.

You shall not steal.

You shall not bear false witness
against your neighbor.

You shall not covet.

16 Jesus answered them, and said, My doctrine is not mine, but his that sent me.

17 If any man will do his will, he shall know of the doctrine, whether it be of God, or whether I speak of myself.

18 He that speaks of himself seeks his own glory: but he that seeks his glory that sent him, the same is true, and no unrighteousness is in him.

19 Did not Moses give you the law, and yet none of you keeps the law? Why do you go about to kill me?

20 The people answered and said, You have a devil: who goes about to kill you?

21 Jesus answered and said to them, I have done one work, and you all marvel.

22 Moses therefore gave to you circumcision; (not because it is of Moses, but of the fathers;) and you on the sabbath day circumcise a man.

23 If a man on the sabbath day receive circumcision, that the law of Moses should not be broken; are you angry at me, because I have made a man every whit whole on the sabbath day?

24 Judge not according to the appearance, but judge righteous judgment.

25 Then said some of them of Jerusalem, Is not this he, whom they seek to kill?

26 But, lo, he speaks boldly, and they say nothing to him. Do the rulers know indeed that this is the very Christ?

27 Howbeit we know this man whence he is: but when Christ comes, no man knows whence he is.

28 Then cried Jesus in the temple as he taught, saying, You both know me, and you know whence I am: and I am not come of myself, but he that sent me is true, whom you know not.

29 But I know him: for I am from him, and he has sent me.

30 Then they sought to take him: but no man laid hands on him, because his hour was not yet come.

31 And many of the people believed on him, and said, When Christ comes, will he do more miracles than these which this man has done?

32 The Pharisees heard that the people murmured such things concerning him; and the Pharisees and the chief priests sent officers to take him.

33 Then said Jesus to them, Yet a little while am I with you, and then I go to him that sent me.

34 You shall seek me, and shall not find me: and where I am, there you cannot come.

35 Then said the Jews among themselves, Where will he go, that we shall not find him? will he go to the dispersed among the Gentiles, and teach the Gentiles?

36 What manner of saying is this that he said, You shall seek me, and shall not find me: and where I am, there you cannot come?

37 In the last day, that great day of the feast, Jesus stood and cried, saying, If any man thirst, let him come to me, and drink.

38 He that believes on me, as the scripture has said, out of his belly shall flow rivers of living water.

39 (But this spoke he of the Spirit, which they that believe on him should receive: for the Holy Spirit was not yet given; because that Jesus was not yet glorified.)

40 Many of the people therefore, when they heard this saying, said, Of a truth this is the Prophet.

41 Others said, This is the Christ. But some said, Shall Christ come out of Galilee?

42 Has not the scripture said, That Christ comes of the seed of David, and out of the town of Bethlehem, where David was?

43 So there was a division among the people because of him.

44 And some of them would have taken him; but no man laid hands on him.

45 Then came the officers to the chief priests and Pharisees; and they said to them, Why have you not brought him?

46 The officers answered, Never man spoke like this man.

47 Then answered them the Pharisees, Are you also deceived?

48 Have any of the rulers or of the Pharisees believed on him?

49 But this people who knows not the law are cursed.

7:37 Salvation is possible for every person. See Acts 2:21.

7:46 The uniqueness of Jesus. "I know men and I tell you that Jesus Christ is no mere man. Between Him and every other person in the world there is no possible term of comparison. Alexander, Caesar, Charlemagne, and I have founded empires. But on what did we rest the creations of our genius? Upon force. Jesus Christ founded His empire upon love; and at this hour millions of men would die for Him." Napoleon Bonaparte (quoted in Evidence That Demands a Verdict by Josh McDowell)

7:52 This showed their ignorance of Scripture (see Isaiah 9:1,2), and of the fact that Jesus was born in Bethlehem.

50 Nicodemus said to them, (he that came to Jesus by night, being one of them,)

51 Does our law judge any man, before it hear him, and know what he does?

52 They answered and said to him, are you also of Galilee? Search, and look: for out of Galilee arises no prophet.

53 And every man went to his own house.

Chapter 8

Jesus went to the mount of Olives.

2 And early in the morning he came again into the temple, and all the people came to him; and he sat down, and taught them.

3 And the scribes and Pharisees brought to him a woman taken in adultery; and when they had set her in the midst,

4 They said to him, Master, this woman was taken in adultery, in the very act.

5 Now Moses in the law commanded us, that such should be stoned: but what do you say?

6 This they said, tempting him, that they might have to accuse him. But Jesus stooped down, and with his finger wrote on the ground, as though he heard them not.

7 So when they continued asking him, he lifted up himself, and said to them, He that is without sin among you, let him first cast a stone at her.

8 And again he stooped down, and wrote on the ground.

9 And they which heard it, being convicted by their own conscience, went out one by one, beginning at the eldest, even to the last: and Jesus was left alone, and the woman standing in the midst.

10 When Jesus had lifted up himself, and saw none but the woman, he said to her, Woman, where are those your accusers? has no man condemned you?

11 She said, No man, Lord. And Jesus said to her, Neither do I condemn you: go, and sin no more.

8:6 It is likely that Jesus wrote the Ten Commandments on the ground. They had been talking about the Law, and each of the men were convicted by their conscience (v. 9), which is the effect of the Law (Romans 2:15). The Law was written in stone (uncompromising), this was written in sand (removable)— besides, what else does God write with His finger? See Exodus 31:18.

Questions & Objections

8:9 **"You are trying to make me feel guilty by quoting the Ten Commandments."**

Ask the person which one of the Ten Commandments makes him feel guilty. Simply state, "The Bible says, 'You shall not steal.' If you feel guilty when you hear that, why do you think that is? Could it be because you are guilty?" God gave us our conscience so we would know when we break His Law; the guilt we feel when we do something wrong tells us that we need to repent. (See also Romans 2:15 comment.)

12 Then spoke Jesus again to them, saying, I am the light of the world: he that follows me shall not walk in darkness, but shall have the light of life.

13 The Pharisees therefore said to him, You bear record of yourself; your record is not true.

14 Jesus answered and said to them, Though I bear record of myself, yet my record is true: for I know whence I came, and where I go; but you cannot tell whence I come, and where I go.

15 You judge after the flesh; I judge no man.

16 And yet if I judge, my judgment is true: for I am not alone, but I and the Father that sent me.

17 It is also written in your law, that the testimony of two men is true.

18 I am one that bears witness of myself, and the Father that sent me bears witness of me.

19 Then said they to him, Where is your Father? Jesus answered, You neither know me, nor my Father: if you had known me, you should have known my Father also.

20 These words spoke Jesus in the treasury, as he taught in the temple: and no man laid hands on him; for his hour was not yet come.

21 Then said Jesus again to them, I go my way, and

Using the Law in Evangelism

8:4,5 The wrath of the Law brought this woman to the feet of the Savior. That's the function of the Law: to condemn. Some may say that we shouldn't condemn anyone, when all the Law does is reveal to the sinner that he is "condemned already" (John 3:18). The Law shows him his danger and therefore his desperate need for the Savior. See Galatians 3:19 comment.

Questions & Objections

8:11   *"Jesus didn't condemn the woman caught in the act of adultery, but condemned those who judged her. Therefore you shouldn't judge other*

The Christian is not "judging others" but simply telling the world of God's judgment—that God (not the Christian) has judged all the world as being guilty before Him (Romans 3:19,23). Jesus was able to offer that woman forgiveness for her sin, because He was on His way to die on the cross for her. She acknowledged Him as "Lord," but He still told her, "Go, and sin no more." If she didn't repent, she would perish.

you shall seek me, and shall die in your sins: where I go, you cannot come.

22   Then said the Jews, Will he kill himself? because he says, Where I go, you cannot come.

23   And he said to them, You are from beneath; I am from above: you are of this world; I am not of this world.

24   I said therefore to you, that you shall die in your sins: for if you believe not that I am he, you shall die in your sins.

25   Then said they to him, Who are thou? And Jesus said to them, Even the same that I said to you from the beginning.

26   I have many things to say and to judge of you: but he that sent me is true; and I speak to the world those things which I have heard of him.

27   They understood not that he spoke to them of the Father.

8:10–12   What a fearful thing it is when we face God's Law. The very stones call for our blood. The Law cries out for justice; it has no mercy. It demands, "The soul that sins shall die!" But the Judge who rules can, at His own discretion, administer the spirit of the Law, and its spirit says that mercy rejoices over judgment—God is rich in mercy to all who call upon Him.

The letter kills, but the Spirit brings life. God is not willing that the wrath of the Law fall upon guilty sinners, because He would rather acquit the criminal from the courtroom...and He can do so because of Calvary.

A. N. Martin said, "The moment God's Law ceases to be the most powerful factor in influencing the moral sensitivity of any individual or nation, there will be indifference to Divine wrath, and when indifference comes in it always brings in its train indifference to salvation."

28 Then said Jesus to them, When you have lifted up the Son of man, then shall you know that I am he, and that I do nothing of myself; but as my Father has taught me, I speak these things.

29 And he that sent me is with me: the Father has not left me alone; for I do always those things that please him.

30 As he spoke these words, many believed on him.

31 Then said Jesus to those Jews which believed on him, If you continue in my word, then are you my disciples indeed;

32 And you shall know the truth, and the truth shall make you free.

33 They answered him, We are Abraham's seed, and were never in bondage to any man: how do you say, You shall be made free?

34 Jesus answered them, Verily, verily, I say to you, Whosoever commits sin is the servant of sin.

35 And the servant abides not in the house for ever: but the Son abides ever.

36 If the Son therefore shall make you free, you shall be free indeed.

37 I know that you are Abraham's seed; but you seek to kill me, because my word has no place in you.

38 I speak that which I have seen with my Father: and you do that which you have seen with your father.

39 They answered and said to him, Abraham is our father. Jesus said to them, If you were Abraham's children, you would do the works of Abraham.

40 But now you seek to kill me, a man that has told you the truth, which I have heard of God: this did not Abraham.

41 You do the deeds of your father. Then said they to him, We are not born of fornication; we have one Father, even God.

42 Jesus said to them, If God were your Father, you would love me: for I proceeded forth and came from God; neither came I of myself, but he sent me.

43 Why do you not understand my speech? even because you cannot hear my word.

44 You are of your father the devil, and the lusts of your father you will do. He was a murderer from the beginning, and abode not in the truth, because there is no truth in him. When he speaks a lie, he speaks of his own: for he is a liar, and the father of it.

45 And because I tell you the truth, you believe me not.

46 Which of you convinces me of sin? And if I say the truth, why do you not believe me?

47 He that is of God hears God's words: you therefore hear them not, because you are not of God.

John 8

48 Then answered the Jews, and said to him, Say we not well that you are a Samaritan, and have a devil?

49 Jesus answered, I have not a devil; but I honor my Father, and you do dishonor me.

50 And I seek not mine own glory: there is one that seeks and judges.

51 Verily, verily, I say to you, If a man keeps my saying, he shall never see death.

52 Then said the Jews to him, Now we know that you have a devil. Abraham is dead, and the prophets; and you say, If a man keeps my saying, he shall never taste of death.

53 Are you greater than our father Abraham, which is dead? and the prophets are dead: whom do you make yourself?

54 Jesus answered, If I honor myself, my honor is nothing: it is my Father that honors me; of whom you say, that he is your God:

8:44 Names of the enemy. The devil is called the god and prince of this world, and the ruler of darkness (2 Corinthians 4:4; John 12:31; Acts 26:18; Ephesians 6:12). He seeks to hinder the work of God and suppress God's Word (Matthew 13:38,39; 1 Thessalonians 2:18). He is a liar, the father of lies, and a murderer (John 8:44). The devil is your adversary and a devourer (1 Peter 5:8). He is the promoter of pride (Genesis 3:5; 1 Timothy 3:6), the stimulator of lust (Ephesians 2:2,3), and the tempter (Luke 4:1–13).

8:51 Jesus' unique words: Anyone who obeys Him would not die. This is not advocating works as a means of salvation, but obedience as a sign of our salvation. We keep His word because we love Him (John 14:23). See 1 John 2:17 and John 8:58 comment.

8:58 Jesus' unique words: Jesus was affirming that He was God manifest in the flesh. He is the Great "I AM"—the Eternal One who revealed Himself to Moses in the burning bush (Exodus 3:14). See John 11:25 comment.

8:58 Was Jesus God in human form? If I give you a small slice of cheese from a large block (the taste being constant throughout the whole block), and you spit out the cheese saying you hate the taste, then you reject the whole block. Jesus was God manifest in human form. If the Jews rejected Him, they rejected the Father also—he who is of God hears God's words. John later stated in his epistle, "Whosoever denies the Son, the same has not the Father: (but) he that acknowledges the Son has the Father also" (1 John 2:23). See John 10:30

55 Yet you have not known him; but I know him: and if I should say, I know him not, I shall be a liar like you: but I know him, and keep his saying.

56 Your father Abraham rejoiced to see my day: and he saw it, and was glad.

57 Then said the Jews to him, You are not yet fifty years old, and have you seen Abraham?

58 Jesus said to them, Verily, verily, I say to you, Before Abraham was, I am.

59 Then took they up stones to cast at him: but Jesus hid himself, and went out of the temple, going through the midst of them, and so passed by.

Chapter 9

And as Jesus passed by, he saw a man which was blind from his birth.

2 And his disciples asked him, saying, Master, who did sin, this man, or his parents, that he was born blind?

3 Jesus answered, Neither has this man sinned, nor his parents: but that the works of God should be made manifest in him.

4 I must work the works of him that sent me, while it is day: the night comes, when no man can work.

5 As long as I am in the world, I am the light of the world.

6 When he had thus spoken, he spat on the ground, and made clay of the spittle, and he anointed the eyes of the blind man with the clay,

7 And said to him, Go, wash in the pool of Siloam, (which is by interpretation, Sent.) He went his way therefore, and washed, and came seeing.

8 The neighbours therefore, and they which before had seen him that he was blind, said, Is not this he that sat and begged?

9 Some said, This is he: others said, He is like him: but he said, I am he.

10 Therefore said they to him, How were your eyes opened?

11 He answered and said, A man that is called Jesus made clay, and anointed mine eyes, and said to me, Go to the pool of Siloam, and wash: and I went and washed, and I received sight.

12 Then said they to him, Where is he? He said, I know not.

13 They brought to the Pharisees him that beforetime was blind.

14 And it was the sabbath day when Jesus made the clay, and opened his eyes.

15 Then again the Pharisees also asked him how he had received his sight. He said to them, He put clay upon mine eyes, and I washed, and do see.

16 Therefore said some of the Pharisees, This man is not of God, because he keeps not the sabbath day. Others said, How can a man that is a sinner do such miracles? And there was a division among them.

17 They said to the blind man again, What do you say of him, that he has opened your eyes? He said, He is a prophet.

18 But the Jews did not believe concerning him, that he had been blind, and received his sight, until they called the parents of him that had received his sight.

19 And they asked them, saying, Is this your son, who you say was born blind? how then does he now see?

20 His parents answered them and said, We know that this is our son, and that he was born blind:

21 But by what means he now sees, we know not; or who has opened his eyes, we know not: he is of age; ask him: he shall speak for himself.

22 These words spoke his parents, because they feared the Jews: for the Jews had agreed already, that if any man did confess that he was Christ, he should be put out of the synagogue.

23 Therefore said his parents, He is of age; ask him.

24 Then again called they the man that was blind, and said to him, Give God the praise: we know that this man is a sinner.

9:4 John Wesley was asked what he would do with his life if he knew that he would die at midnight the next day. His answer was something like this: "I would just carry on with what I am doing. I will arise at 5:00 a.m. for prayer, then take a house meeting at 6.00 a.m. At 12 noon, I will be preaching at an open-air. At 3:00 p.m. I have another meeting in another town. At 6:00 p.m. I have a house meeting; at 10:00 p.m. I have a prayer meeting and at 12:00 midnight, I would go to be with my Lord."

If we knew we were to die at 12 o'clock tomorrow night, would we have to step up our evangelistic efforts, or could we in all good conscience carry on just as we are?

"The evangelistic harvest is always urgent. The destiny of men and of nations is always being decided. Every generation is strategic. We are not responsible for the past generation, and we cannot bear the full responsibility for the next one; but we do have our generation. God will hold us responsible as to how well we fulfill our responsibilities to this age and take advantage of our opportunities." Billy Graham

25 He answered and said, Whether he be a sinner or no, I know not: one thing I know, that, whereas I was blind, now I see.

26 Then said they to him again, What did he to you? how opened he your eyes?

27 He answered them, I have told you already, and you did not hear: wherefore would you hear it again? will you also be his disciples?

28 Then they reviled him, and said, You are his disciple; but we are Moses' disciples.

29 We know that God spoke to Moses: as for this fellow, we know not from whence he is.

30 The man answered and said to them, Why herein is a marvelous thing, that you know not from whence he is, and yet he has opened mine eyes.

31 Now we know that God hears not sinners: but if any man be a worshipper of God, and does his will, him he hears.

32 Since the world began was it not heard that any man opened the eyes of one that was born blind.

33 If this man were not of God, he could do nothing.

34 They answered and said to him, You were altogether born in sins, and do you teach us? And they cast him out.

35 Jesus heard that they had cast him out; and when he had found him, he said to him, Do you believe on the Son of God?

36 He answered and said, Who is he, Lord, that I might believe on him?

The Function of the Law

9:7 When we apply the tablets of the Law to the eyes of sinners, it causes them to have reason to go to the cleansing pool of the gospel. This man would not have had a reason to go to the pool, until he perceived that he was unclean. That's the function of the Law—to convince a man he is unclean (Romans 7:13). Charles Spurgeon said, "No man will ever put on the robe of Christ's righteousness till he is stripped of his fig leaves, nor will he wash in the fount of mercy till he perceives his filthiness. Therefore, my brethren, we must not cease to declare the Law, its demands, its threatenings, and the sinner's multiplied breaches of it."

9:25 This is the testimony of the newly saved. There are many questions for which they have no answers. But one thing they do know: "Whereas I was blind, now I see." It has been well said that the man with an experience is not at the mercy of a man with an argument.

37 And Jesus said to him, You have both seen him, and it is he that talks with you.

38 And he said, Lord, I believe. And he worshipped him.

39 And Jesus said, For judgment I am come into this world, that they which see not might see; and that they which see might be made blind.

40 And some of the Pharisees which were with him heard these words, and said to him, Are we blind also?

41 Jesus said to them, If you were blind, you should have no sin: but now you say, We see; therefore your sin remains.

Chapter 10

Verily, verily, I say to you, He that enters not by the door into the sheepfold, but climbs up some other way, the same is a thief and a robber.

2　But he that enters in by the door is the shepherd of the sheep.

3　To him the porter opens; and the sheep hear his voice: and he calls his own sheep by name, and leads them out.

4　And when he puts forth his own sheep, he goes before them, and the sheep follow him: for they know his voice.

5　And a stranger will they not follow, but will flee from him: for they know not the voice of strangers.

6　This parable spoke Jesus to them: but they understood not what things they were which he spoke to them.

7　Then said Jesus to them again, Verily, verily, I say to you, I am the door of the sheep.

8　All that ever came before me are thieves and robbers: but the sheep did not hear them.

9　I am the door: by me if any man enter in, he shall be saved, and shall go in and out, and find pasture.

10　The thief comes not, but for to steal, and to kill, and to destroy: I am come that they might have life, and that they might have it more abundantly.

10:2 True believers are likened to sheep, which: know the voice of their shepherd; are easily led (they submit without resistance); flock together (in unity); need a shepherd (or they stray); were a type of Israel (Matthew 10:6); imitate one another; are productive (wool, leather, meat, and milk); were a sign of God's blessing (see Deuteronomy 7:13); will be divided from the "goats" at the Judgment; were offered in sacrifice.

11 I am the good shepherd: the good shepherd gives his life for the sheep.

12 But he that is an hireling, and not the shepherd, whose own the sheep are not, sees the wolf coming, and leaves the sheep, and flees: and the wolf catches them, and scatters the sheep.

13 The hireling flees, because he is an hireling, and cares not for the sheep.

10:9 A Hebrew servant who was given his freedom had the option to stay with a master he loved. If he chose to give up his freedom, his master took him to the doorpost and pierced his ear with an awl, "and he shall serve him forever" (Exodus 21:5,6). In the same way, the sinner, upon conversion, is given freedom from sin and becomes a servant of Jesus Christ (1 Corinthians 7:22), to serve Him forever. He presents his body as a living sacrifice. His ear is forever open to the Door of the Savior (John 10:9).

10:10 "Evangelism is about experiencing God. If you choose to be obedient, He will take you on a journey so exciting that your life will never be the same." Bill Fay, Share Jesus Without Fear

"Evangelism is the cure to the disease of church boredom." Todd P. McCollum

"I can tell you that there is no greater joy than leading someone to faith in Jesus Christ. Even if they reject your message, it still feels great to obey Christ. Yet regardless of how we feel, we need to remember this is what He has commanded." D. James Kennedy

10:11 Hundreds of years earlier, David had written that the Lord was his shepherd, and now that Shepherd had become flesh. Here is a continuance of the most famous of psalms, Psalm 23. This was the "Great Shepherd" Himself (Hebrews 13:20), the One who takes away the "want" of the covetous human heart. He was the path of righteousness, who brought light to the valley of the shadow of death. Here was the Bread of Life, placed by God on a table in the presence of our enemies. Heaven's cup "ran over," and brought the Father's goodness and mercy to us, so that we might dwell in the House of the Lord forever.

10:16 The Mormons misrepresent this verse. It is an obvious reference to the Gentiles. See John 11:52; Romans 15:9–12; Ephesians 2:11–18.

14 I am the good shepherd, and know my sheep, and am known of mine.

15 As the Father knows me, even so know I the Father: and I lay down my life for the sheep.

16 And other sheep I have, which are not of this fold: them also I must bring, and they shall hear my voice; and there shall be one fold, and one shepherd.

17 Therefore does my Father love me, because I lay down my life, that I might take it again.

18 No man takes it from me, but I lay it down of myself. I have power to lay it down, and I have power to take it again. This commandment have I received of my Father.

19 There was a division therefore again among the Jews for these sayings.

20 And many of them said, He has a devil, and is mad; why do you hear him?

21 Others said, These are not the words of him that has a devil. Can a devil open the eyes of the blind?

22 And it was at Jerusalem the feast of the dedication, and it was winter.

23 And Jesus walked in the temple in Solomon's porch.

24 Then came the Jews round about him, and said to him, How long do you make us to doubt? If you be the Christ, tell us plainly.

25 Jesus answered them, I told you, and you believed not: the works that I do in my Father's name, they bear witness of me.

26 But you believe not, because you are not of my sheep, as I said to you.

27 My sheep hear my voice, and I know them, and they follow me:

28 And I give to them eternal life; and they shall never perish, neither shall any man pluck them out of my hand.

29 My Father, which gave them me, is greater than all; and no man is able to pluck them out of my Father's hand.

30 I and my Father are one.

31 Then the Jews took up stones again to stone him.

10:27 See 2 Timothy 2:19 comment.

10:30 Was Jesus God in human form? See John 10:38.

10:38 Was Jesus God in human form? See John 14:10.

32 Jesus answered them, Many good works have I showed you from my Father; for which of those works do you stone me?

33 The Jews answered him, saying, For a good work we stone you not; but for blasphemy; and because that you, being a man, make yourself God.

34 Jesus answered them, Is it not written in your law, I said, You are gods?

35 If he called them gods, to whom the word of God came, and the scripture cannot be broken;

36 Do you say of him, whom the Father has sanctified, and sent into the world, You blaspheme; because I said, I am the Son of God?

The Bible is unique and proves itself to be supernatural in origin.

37 If I do not the works of my Father, believe me not.

38 But if I do, though you believe not me, believe the works: that you may know, and believe, that the Father is in me, and I in him.

39 Therefore they sought again to take him: but he escaped out of their hand,

40 And went away again beyond Jordan into the place where John at first baptized; and there he abode.

41 And many resorted to him, and said, John did no miracle: but all things that John spoke of this man were true.

42 And many believed on him there.

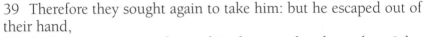

Chapter 11

Now a certain man was sick, named Lazarus, of Bethany, the town of Mary and her sister Martha.

2 (It was that Mary which anointed the Lord with ointment, and wiped his feet with her hair, whose brother Lazarus was sick.)

3 Therefore his sisters sent to him, saying, Lord, behold, he whom you love is sick.

4 When Jesus heard that, he said, This sickness is not to death, but for the glory of God, that the Son of God might be glorified thereby.

5 Now Jesus loved Martha, and her sister, and Lazarus.

6 When he had heard therefore that he was sick, he abode two days still in the same place where he was.

10:36

The Deity of Jesus

Fom *Christ Before the Manger* by Ron Rhodes
A strong argument for the deity of Christ is the fact that many of the names, titles, and attributes ascribed to Yehweh are also ascribed to Jesus Christ

Description	Father	Jesus
Yahweh ("I AM")	Exodus 3:14 Deuteronomy 32:39 Isaiah 43:10	John 8:24 John 8:58 John 18:4–6
God	Genesis 1:1 Deuteronomy 6:4 Psalm 45:6,7	Isaiah 7:14 Isaiah 9:6 John 1:1,14 John 20:28 Titus 2:13 Hebrews 1:8 2 Peter 1:1 Matthew 1:23 1 John 5:20
Alpha and Omega (First and Last)	Isaiah 41:4 Isaiah 48:12 Revelation 1:8	Revelation 1:17,18 Revelation 2:8 Revelation 22:12–16
Lord	Isaiah 45:23	Matthew 12:8 Acts 7:59,60 Acts 10:36 Romans 10:12 1 Corinthians 2:8 1 Corinthians 12:3 Philippians 2:10,11
Savior	Isaiah 43:3 Isaiah 43:11 Isaiah 49:26 Isaiah 63:8 Luke 1:47 1 Timothy 4:10	Matthew 1:21 Luke 2:11 John 1:29 John 4:42 2 Timothy 1:10 Titus 2:13 Hebrews 5:9
King	Psalm 95:3 Isaiah 43:15 Timothy 6:14–16	Revelation 17:14 Revelation 19:16

Description	Father	Jesus
Judge	Genesis 18:25 Deuteronomy 32:36 Psalm 50:4,6; 96:13 Psalm 58:11; 75;7	John 5:22 2 Corinthians 5:10 2 Timothy 4:1
Light	2 Samuel 22:29 Psalm 27:1	John 1:4,9 John 3:19 John 8:12 John 9:5
Rock 10:3,4	Deuteronomy 32:3,4 2 Samuel 22:32 Psalm 89:26	Romans 9:33 1 Corinthians 1 Peter 2:4–8
Redeemer	Psalm 130:7,8 Isaiah 43:1 Isaiah 48:17 Isaiah 49:26 Isaiah 54:5	Acts 20:28 Ephesians 1:7 Hebrews 9:12
Our Righteousness	Isaiah 45:24	Jeremiah 23:6 Romans 3:21,22
Husband	Isaiah 54:5 Hosea 2:16	Matthew 25:1 Mark 2:18,19 2 Corinthians 11:2 Ephesians 5:25–32 Revelation 21:2,9
Shepherd	Genesis 49:24 Psalm 23:1 Psalm 80:1	John 10:11,16 Hebrews 13:20 1 Peter 2:25 1 Peter 5:4
Creator	Genesis 1:1 Job 33:4 Psalm 95:5,6 Psalm 102:24,25 Isaiah 40:28 Isaiah 43:1 Acts 4:24	John 1:2,3,10 Colossians 1:15–18 Hebrews 1:1–3,10

Description	Father	Jesus
Giver of Life	Genesis 2:7 Deuteronomy 32:39 1 Samuel 2:6 Psalm 36:9	John 5:21 John 10:28 John 11:25
Forgiver of Sin	Exodus 34:6,7 Nehemiah 9:17 Daniel 9:9 Jonah 4:2	Matthew 9:2 Mark 2:1–12 Acts 26:18 Colossians 2:13 Colossians 3:13
Lord our Healer	Exodus 15:26	Acts 9:34
Omnipresent	Psalm 139:7–12 Proverbs 15:3	Matthew 18:20 Matthew 28:20 Ephesians 3:17 Ephesians 4:10
Omniscient	1 Kings 8:39 Jeremiah 17:10,16	Matthew 9:4 Matthew 11:27 Luke 5:4–6 John 2:25 John 16:30 John 21:17 Acts 1:24
Omnipotent	Isaiah 40:10–31 Isaiah 45:5–13 Revelation 19:6	Matthew 28:18 Mark 1:29–34 John 10:18 Jude 24
Preexistent	Genesis 1:1	John 1:15,30 John 3:13,31,32 John 6:62 John 16:28 John 17:5
Eternal	Psalm 102:26,27 Habakkuk 3:6	Isaiah 9:6 Micah 5:2 John 8:58
Immutable	Malachi 3:6 James 1:17	Hebrews 13:8

Description	Father	Jesus
Receiver of worship	Matthew 4:10 John 4:24 Revelation 5:14 Revelation 7:11 Revelation 11:16 Revelation 19:4,10	Matthew 2:8,11 Matthew 14:33 Matthew 28:9 John 9:38 Philippians 2:10,11 Hebrews 1:6
Hope Speaker with divine authority	Jeremiah 17:7 "Thus saith the Lord..." —used hundreds of times	1 Timothy 1:1 Matthew 23:34–37 John 3:5 John 7:46 "Truly, truly, I say..."
Who raised Jesus from the dead?	Acts 2:24,32 Romans 8:11 1 Corinthians 6:14	John 2:19–22 John 10:17,18 Matthew 27:40
Who gets the glory?	Isaiah 42:8 Isaiah 48:11	Hebrews 13:21 John 17:5

7   Then after that said he to his disciples, Let us go into Judea again.

8   His disciples said to him, Master, the Jews of late sought to stone you; and you go there again?

9   Jesus answered, Are there not twelve hours in the day? If any man walk in the day, he stumbles not, because he sees the light of this world.

10   But if a man walk in the night, he stumbles, because there is no light in him.

11   These things said he: and after that he said to them, Our friend Lazarus sleeps; but I go, that I may awake him out of sleep.

12   Then said his disciples, Lord, if he sleep, he shall do well.

11:6 God's ways are distinctively and consistently different from ours. God did not rescue Daniel out of the lion's den as we would have. He didn't turn off the fiery furnace into which Shadrach, Meshach, and Abed-Nego were cast, as we would. He didn't kill Pharaoh and save the Israelites from the Red Sea; instead He worked His wondrous purposes in the lion's den, in the furnace, and in the Red Sea. Lion's teeth, fire, and water are no big deal to the God who created them. Death, at the presence of the Light of the world, is but a shadow that quickly dissipates like a frightened and sickly child.

13 Howbeit Jesus spoke of his death: but they thought that he had spoken of taking of rest in sleep.

14 Then said Jesus to them plainly, Lazarus is dead.

15 And I am glad for your sakes that I was not there, to the intent you may believe; nevertheless let us go to him.

16 Then said Thomas, which is called Didymus, to his fellow-disciples, Let us also go, that we may die with him.

17 Then when Jesus came, he found that he had lain in the grave four days already.

18 Now Bethany was near to Jerusalem, about fifteen furlongs off:

19 And many of the Jews came to Martha and Mary, to comfort them concerning their brother.

20 Then Martha, as soon as she heard that Jesus was coming, went and met him: but Mary sat still in the house.

21 Then said Martha to Jesus, Lord, if you had been here, my brother had not died.

22 But I know, that even now, whatsoever you will ask of God, God will give it you.

23 Jesus said to her, Your brother shall rise again.

11:25 The uniqueness of Jesus. "A man who was merely a man and said the sort of things Jesus said wouldn't be a great moral teacher. He'd either be a lunatic—on a level with the man who says he's a poached egg—or else he'd be the Devil of Hell. You must make your choice. Either this man was, and is, the Son of God: or else a madman or something worse. You can shut Him up for a fool, you can spit at Him and kill Him as a demon; or you can fall at His feet and call Him Lord and God. But don't let us come with any patronizing nonsense about His being a great human teacher. He hasn't left that open to us. He didn't intend to." C. S. Lewis, *The Case for Christianity*

11:25 Jesus' unique words: See John 14:6 comment.

11:35 In one sense, this verse is a mystery because Jesus knew what He was about to do. He was about to give Mary and Martha the greatest gift, outside of salvation, that they could ever hope for. Yet, He wept.

The prophets tell us that the Messiah would be a "man of sorrows, and acquainted with grief" (Isaiah 53:3). He was moved with compassion for the multitudes, wept over Jerusalem, and knew what it was to "weep with those who weep." Even though we have heaven before us, it pains the Head of the Body when the foot hurts. Jesus is a High Priest who is "touched with the feeling of our infirmities" (Hebrews 4:15).

11:14 How to Preach at a Funeral for Someone You Suspect Died Unsaved

By Mike Smalley

1. Start in the natural realm and swing to the spiritual.

2. Say something positive about the person who has died—either personally, or their marriage, kids, work ethic, their generation, etc. This should build rapport with the audience. Use a humorous story that relates to the above.

3. Don't feel pressured to mention where the deceased may have gone after death (God is the only One who truly knows).

4. Never insinuate that he went to heaven.

5. Use this as a springboard: "Good friends often remind us of things that we don't want to deal with, but that are very important. Bob, today, reminds us that we all must die."

6. Use anecdotes that convey eternal truths.

7. Go quickly but thoroughly through each of the Ten Commandments.

8. Warn briefly about sin, death, judgment, and eternity.

9. Give a clear gospel presentation.

10. Appeal to the audience to repent today.

"When anyone dies, I ask myself, 'Was I faithful?' Did I speak all the truth? And did I speak it from my very soul every time I preached?"
Charles Spurgeon

24 Martha said to him, I know that he shall rise again in the resurrection at the last day.

25 Jesus said to her, I am the resurrection, and the life: he that believes in me, though he were dead, yet shall he live:

26 And whosoever lives and believes in me shall never die. Do you believe this?

27 She said to him, Yea, Lord: I believe that you are the Christ, the Son of God, which should come into the world.

28 And when she had so said, she went her way, and called Mary her sister secretly, saying, The Master is come, and calls for you.

29 As soon as she heard that, she arose quickly, and came to him.

30 Now Jesus was not yet come into the town, but was in that place where Martha met him.

31 The Jews then which were with her in the house, and comforted her, when they saw Mary, that she rose up hastily and went out, followed her, saying, She goes to the grave to weep there.

32 Then when Mary was come where Jesus was, and saw him, she fell down at his feet, saying to him, Lord, if you had been here, my brother had not died.

33 When Jesus therefore saw her weeping, and the Jews also weeping which came with her, he groaned in the spirit, and was troubled,

34 And said, Where have you laid him? They said to him, Lord, come and see.

35 Jesus wept.

36 Then said the Jews, Behold how he loved him!

37 And some of them said, Could not this man, which opened the eyes of the blind, have caused that even this man should not have died?

38 Jesus therefore again groaning in himself came to the grave. It was a cave, and a stone lay upon it.

11:43,44 The words of Jesus cut through the icy grip of death like a white-hot blade through soft powdered snow. The same Word that brought life in the beginning breathed life into the decomposing corpse of Lazarus. Suddenly, from the blackened shadow of the tomb appeared a figure, wrapped in grave clothes. As he stood at the entrance of the tomb (for tombs didn't need an exit until that day), his face and body were covered with grave clothes. God took him by the hand and led him to the light.

What a picture of what is before us! The hour is coming when all who are in their graves will hear His voice. The victory Lazarus had over death was bad news for the devil and the undertaker, but it was only a temporary triumph, for the undertaker would eventually get his deathly fee. Lazarus would ultimately depart from this earth, but the time is coming when death shall be no more. On that day, we will exchange these vile, perishing bodies for incorruptible bodies that will never feel pain, disease, or death:

> *"So when this corruptible shall have put on incorruption, and this mortal shall have put on immortality, then shall be brought to pass the saying that is written, Death is swallowed up in victory"* (1 Corinthians 15:54).

For those who trust in Jesus, this body is but a chrysalis, which may become wrinkled and crusty with age, but it is just a shell that will be dropped off as the new butterfly emerges.

39 Jesus said, Take away the stone. Martha, the sister of him that was dead, said to him, Lord, by this time he stinks: for he has been dead four days.

40 Jesus said to her, Said I not to you, that, if you would believe, you should see the glory of God?

41 Then they took away the stone from the place where the dead was laid. And Jesus lifted up his eyes, and said, Father, I thank you that you have heard me.

42 And I knew that you hear me always: but because of the people which stand by I said it, that they may believe that you have sent me.

43 And when he thus had spoken, he cried with a loud voice, Lazarus, come forth.

44 And he that was dead came forth, bound hand and foot with graveclothes: and his face was bound about with a napkin. Jesus said to them, Loose him, and let him go.

45 Then many of the Jews which came to Mary, and had seen the things which Jesus did, believed on him.

46 But some of them went their ways to the Pharisees, and told them what things Jesus had done.

47 Then gathered the chief priests and the Pharisees a council, and said, What do we? for this man does many miracles.

48 If we let him thus alone, all men will believe on him: and the Romans shall come and take away both our place and nation.

49 And one of them, named Caiaphas, being the high priest that same year, said to them, You know nothing at all,

50 Nor consider that it is expedient for us, that one man should die for the people, and that the whole nation perish not.

51 And this spoke he not of himself: but being high priest that year, he prophesied that Jesus should die for that nation;

52 And not for that nation only, but that also he should gather together in one the children of God that were scattered abroad.

53 Then from that day forth they took counsel together for to put him to death.

54 Jesus therefore walked no more openly among the Jews; but went thence to a country near to the wilderness, into a city called Ephraim, and there continued with his disciples.

55 And the Jews' passover was near at hand: and many went out of the country up to Jerusalem before the passover, to purify themselves.

56 Then sought they for Jesus, and spoke among themselves, as they stood in the temple, What do you think, that he will not come to the feast?

57 Now both the chief priests and the Pharisees had given a commandment, that, if any man knew where he were, he should show it, that they might take him.

Chapter 12

Then Jesus six days before the passover came to Bethany, where Lazarus was which had been dead, whom he raised from the dead.

2 There they made him a supper; and Martha served: but Lazarus was one of them that sat at the table with him.

3 Then took Mary a pound of ointment of spikenard, very costly, and anointed the feet of Jesus, and wiped his feet with her hair: and the house was filled with the odor of the ointment.

4 Then said one of his disciples, Judas Iscariot, Simon's son, which should betray him,

5 Why was not this ointment sold for three hundred pence, and given to the poor?

6 This he said, not that he cared for the poor; but because he was a thief, and had the bag, and bare what was put therein.

7 Then said Jesus, Let her alone: against the day of my burying has she kept this.

8 For the poor always you have with you; but me you have not always.

9 Much people of the Jews therefore knew that he was there: and they came not for Jesus' sake only, but that they might see Lazarus also, whom he had raised from the dead.

10 But the chief priests consulted that they might put Lazarus also to death;

11 Because that by reason of him many of the Jews went away, and believed on Jesus.

12 On the next day much people that were come to the feast, when they heard that Jesus was coming to Jerusalem,

13 Took branches of palm trees, and went forth to meet him, and cried, Hosanna: Blessed is the King of Israel that comes in the name of the Lord.

14 And Jesus, when he had found a young ass, sat thereon; as it is written,

15 Fear not, daughter of Zion: behold, your King comes, sitting on an ass's colt.

16 These things understood not his disciples at the first: but when Jesus was glorified, then remembered they that these things were written of him, and that they had done these things to him.

17 The people therefore that was with him when he called Lazarus out of his grave, and raised him from the dead, bare record.

18 For this cause the people also met him, for that they heard that he had done this miracle.

19 The Pharisees therefore said among themselves, Perceive how you prevail nothing? behold, the world is gone after him.

20 And there were certain Greeks among them that came up to worship at the feast:

21 The same came therefore to Philip, which was of Bethsaida of Galilee, and desired him, saying, Sir, we would see Jesus.

22 Philip came and told Andrew: and again Andrew and Philip tell Jesus.

12:9 The undertaker's nightmare. The Son of God created havoc for undertakers by speaking to their frigid merchandise. His voice was supernatural. A mere "Lazarus, come forth," spoken to a corpse meant a nightmarish dilemma for the Bethany funeral director, because he was left with no body to deal with. Up until that moment, his business was mortally secure. Four days after the death, he had everything wrapped up, when suddenly, three words unraveled his inanimate toil. Reimbursement of all funeral expenses was just the beginning of the bad dream. Death was his living, and if this stranger from Nazareth continued to speak around graves, his business itself would soon be terminal. Jesus Christ was the undertaker's nightmare because death bowed its vile knee to His voice, and the day is promised when all undertakers will hit the unemployment line!

The raising of Lazarus snatched the profit from the undertaker; but the incident happened for the inestimable profit of humanity. It was the long-awaited fulfillment of what was spoken of by the prophets of old. It was a beam of wondrous and glistening light in the most hopeless and darkest of all caves.

12:14 Instead of riding triumphantly through the streets of Jerusalem on a kingly white stallion, He chose to ride on a young donkey, a lowly beast of burden. Imagine how humbling it would be for the president of the United States to ride through New York on the back of a donkey. But this is what the King of kings did. This time He came in lowliness, humbling Himself and becoming obedient to the death of the cross. The next time He will come in flaming fire, on a white horse with ten thousands of His saints.

23 And Jesus answered them, saying, The hour is come, that the Son of man should be glorified.

24 Verily, verily, I say to you, Except a corn of wheat fall into the ground and die, it abides alone: but if it die, it brings forth much fruit.

25 He that loves his life shall lose it; and he that hates his life in this world shall keep it to life eternal.

26 If any man serve me, let him follow me; and where I am, there shall also my servant be: if any man serve me, him will my Father honor.

27 Now is my soul troubled; and what shall I say? Father, save me from this hour: but for this cause came I to this hour.

28 Father, glorify your name. Then came there a voice from heaven, saying, I have both glorified it, and will glorify it again.

> Men have been helped to live by remembering that they must die.
>
> Charles Spurgeon

29 The people therefore, that stood by, and heard it, said that it thundered: others said, An angel spoke to him.

30 Jesus answered and said, This voice came not because of me, but for your sakes.

31 Now is the judgment of this world: now shall the prince of this world be cast out.

32 And I, if I be lifted up from the earth, will draw all men to me.

33 This he said, signifying what death he should die.

34 The people answered him, We have heard out of the law that Christ abides for ever: and how do you say, The Son of man must be lifted up? who is this Son of man?

35 Then Jesus said to them, Yet a little while is the light with you. Walk while you have the light, lest darkness come upon you: for he that walks in darkness knows not where he goes.

36 While you have light, believe in the light, that you may be the children of light. These things spoke Jesus, and departed, and did hide himself from them.

37 But though he had done so many miracles before them, yet they believed not on him:

12:25 "The greatest proof of Christianity for others is not how far a man can logically analyze his reasons for believing, but how far in practice he will stake his life on his belief." T. S. Eliot

12:38 One would think that a terminally ill world would gladly embrace the cure of the gospel, but few, so few believe our report.

38 That the saying of Isaiah the prophet might be fulfilled, which he spoke, Lord, who has believed our report? and to whom has the arm of the Lord been revealed?

39 Therefore they could not believe, because that Isaiah said again,

40 He has blinded their eyes, and hardened their heart; that they should not see with their eyes, nor understand with their heart, and be converted, and I should heal them.

41 These things said Isaiah, when he saw his glory, and spoke of him.

42 Nevertheless among the chief rulers also many believed on him; but because of the Pharisees they did not confess him, lest they should be put out of the synagogue:

43 For they loved the praise of men more than the praise of God.

44 Jesus cried and said, He that believes on me, believes not on me, but on him that sent me.

45 And he that sees me sees him that sent me.

46 I am come a light into the world, that whosoever believes on me should not abide in darkness.

47 And if any man hear my words, and believe not, I judge him not: for I came not to judge the world, but to save the world.

48 He that rejects me, and receives not my words, has one that judges him: the word that I have spoken, the same shall judge him in the last day.

49 For I have not spoken of myself; but the Father which sent me, he gave me a commandment, what I should say, and what I should speak.

50 And I know that his commandment is life everlasting: whatsoever I speak therefore, even as the Father said to me, so I speak.

Chapter 13

Now before the feast of the passover, when Jesus knew that his hour was come that he should depart out of this world to the Father, having loved his own which were in the world, he loved them to the end.

2 And supper being ended, the devil having now put into the heart of Judas Iscariot, Simon's son, to betray him;

3 Jesus knowing that the Father had given all things into his hands, and that he was come from God, and went to God;

4 He rose from supper, and laid aside his garments; and took a towel, and girded himself.

5   After that he poured water into a basin, and began to wash the disciples' feet, and to wipe them with the towel wherewith he was girded.

6   Then came he to Simon Peter: and Peter said to him, Lord, do you wash my feet?

7   Jesus answered and said to him, What I do you know not now; but you shall know hereafter.

8   Peter said to him, You shall never wash my feet. Jesus answered him, If I wash you not, you have no part with me.

9   Simon Peter said to him, Lord, not my feet only, but also my hands and my head.

10   Jesus said to him, He that is washed needs not save to wash his feet, but is clean every whit: and you are clean, but not all.

11   For he knew who should betray him; therefore said he, You are not all clean.

12   So after he had washed their feet, and had taken his garments, and was set down again, he said to them, Do you know what I have done to you?

13   You call me Master and Lord: and you say well; for so I am.

14   If I then, your Lord and Master, have washed your feet; you also ought to wash one another's feet.

15   For I have given you an example, that you should do as I have done to you.

16   Verily, verily, I say to you, The servant is not greater than his lord; neither he that is sent greater than he that sent him.

17   If you know these things, happy are you if you do them.

18   I speak not of you all: I know whom I have chosen: but that the scripture may be fulfilled, He that eats bread with me has lifted up his heel against me.

13:2 While "the devil made me do it" will not be a valid defense on Judgment Day, if more people would believe that the devil is at work in their lives, our prisons would be less full and human suffering would be much less.

So often we hear of people feeling "compelled" to kill, and thinking the impulses were their own. If potential homosexuals understood the influence of unclean spirits, they would be less likely to follow every grimy impulse that comes into their minds. Those who believe that our battle is not against flesh and blood, but demonic personalities, will then be less prone to be tools of darkness.

19 Now I tell you before it come, that, when it is come to pass, you may believe that I am he.

20 Verily, verily, I say to you, He that receives whomsoever I send receives me; and he that receives me receives him that sent me.

21 When Jesus had thus said, he was troubled in spirit, and testified, and said, Verily, verily, I say to you, that one of you shall betray me.

22 Then the disciples looked one on another, doubting of whom he spoke.

23 Now there was leaning on Jesus' bosom one of his disciples, whom Jesus loved.

24 Simon Peter therefore beckoned to him, that he should ask who it should be of whom he spoke.

25 He then lying on Jesus' breast said to him, Lord, who is it?

26 Jesus answered, He it is, to whom I shall give a sop, when I have dipped it. And when he had dipped the sop, he gave it to Judas Iscariot, the son of Simon.

27 And after the sop Satan entered into him. Then said Jesus to him, That you do, do quickly.

28 Now no man at the table knew for what intent he spoke this to him.

29 For some of them thought, because Judas had the bag, that Jesus had said to him, Buy those things that we have need of against the feast; or, that he should give something to the poor.

30 He then having received the sop went immediately out: and it was night.

31 Therefore, when he was gone out, Jesus said, Now is the Son of man glorified, and God is glorified in him.

32 If God be glorified in him, God shall also glorify him in himself, and shall straightway glorify him.

33 Little children, yet a little while I am with you. You shall seek me: and as I said to the Jews, Where I go, you cannot come; so now I say to you.

34 A new commandment I give to you, That you love one another; as I have loved you, that you also love one another.

35 By this shall all men know that you are my disciples, if you have love one to another.

36 Simon Peter said to him, Lord, where are you going? Jesus answered him, Where I go, you can not follow me now; but you shall follow me afterwards.

37 Peter said to him, Lord, why cannot I follow you now? I will lay down my life for your sake.

38 Jesus answered him, Will you lay down your life for my sake? Verily, verily, I say to you, The cock shall not crow, till you have denied me thrice.

Chapter 14

Let not your heart be troubled: you believe in God, believe also in me.

2 In my Father's house are many mansions: if it were not so, I would have told you. I go to prepare a place for you.

3   And if I go and prepare a place for you, I will come again, and receive you to myself; that where I am, there you may be also.

4   And where I go you know, and the way you know.

5   Thomas said to him, Lord, we know not where you go; and how can we know the way?

6   Jesus said to him, I am the way, the truth, and the life: no man comes to the Father, but by me.

7   If you had known me, you should have known my Father also: and from henceforth you know him, and have seen him.

8   Philip said to him, Lord, show us the Father, and it suffices us.

9   Jesus said to him, Have I been so long time with you, and yet have you not known me, Philip? he that has seen me has seen the Father; and how do you say then, Show us the Father?

10 Do you not believe that I am in the Father, and the Father in me? the words that I speak to you I speak not of myself: but the Father that dwells in me, he does the works.

11   Believe me that I am in the Father, and the Father in me: or else believe me for the very works' sake.

12   Verily, verily, I say to you, He that believes on me, the works that I do shall he do also; and greater works than these shall he do; because I go to my Father.

13   And whatsoever you shall ask in my name, that will I do, that the Father may be glorified in the Son.

14:2   Faith in God clears the muddy waters of fear. The Christian who has confidence in Jesus Christ knows that his eternal footsteps have been ordered by the Lord, and that there is a mansion prepared for him that his wildest imaginations could not conceive. If these things weren't so, Jesus would have told us. He is not a liar. His word is sure and steadfast, a mooring for the soul, and those who come into the harbor of a calm faith in God have perfect peace in the troubled storms of this world.

14 If you shall ask any thing in my name, I will do it.

15 If you love me, keep my commandments.

16 And I will pray the Father, and he shall give you another Comforter, that he may abide with you for ever;

17 Even the Spirit of truth; whom the world cannot receive, because it sees him not, neither knows him: but you know him; for he dwells with you, and shall be in you.

18 I will not leave you comfortless: I will come to you.

19 Yet a little while, and the world sees me no more; but you see me: because I live, you shall live also.

20 At that day you shall know that I am in my Father, and you in me, and I in you.

21 He that has my commandments, and keeps them, he it is that loves me: and he that loves me shall be loved of my Father, and I will love him, and will manifest myself to him.

22 Judas said to him, not Iscariot, Lord, how is it that you will manifest yourself to us, and not to the world?

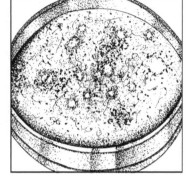

The Bible gives instructions on how to avoid diseases, thousands of years before man discovered their cause. See Hebrews 11:3 comment.

23 Jesus answered and said to him, If a man love me, he will keep my words: and my Father will love him, and we will come to him, and make our abode with him.

24 He that loves me not keeps not my sayings: and the word which you hear is not mine, but the Father's which sent me.

25 These things have I spoken to you, being yet present with you.

26 But the Comforter, which is the Holy Spirit, whom the Father will send in my name, he shall teach you all things, and bring all things to your remembrance, whatsoever I have said to you.

27 Peace I leave with you, my peace I give to you: not as the world gives, give I to you. Let not your heart be troubled, neither let it be afraid.

28 You have heard how I said to you, I go away, and come again to you. If you loved me, you would rejoice, because I said, I go to the Father: for my Father is greater than I.

29 And now I have told you before it come to pass, that, when it is come to pass, you might believe.

Questions & Objections

14:6 "It's intolerant to say that Jesus is the only way to God!"

Jesus is the One who said that He is the only way to the Father. For Christians to say that there are other ways to find peace with God is to bear false testimony. In one sweeping statement, Jesus discards all other religions as a means of finding forgiveness of sins. This agrees with other Scriptures: "Neither is there salvation in any other: for there is no other name under heaven given among men, whereby we must be saved" (Acts 4:12), and "For there is one God, and one mediator between God and men, the man Christ Jesus" (1 Timothy 2:5).

14:6 Jesus' unique words: Paige Patterson stated, "It comes down to a question of truth. Every false religious expression is a religion of darkness. That doesn't mean there are no good things in that faith. But if Jesus is to be taken seriously when He says, 'No one comes to the Father but through Me,' every other proposal is one of darkness." See John 14:21 comment.

14:10 Was Jesus God in human form? See John 17:22.

14:14 In 1 Kings 3:5, the Lord appeared to Solomon in a dream by night, and said, "Ask! What shall I give you?" God asks us the same question. Be like Solomon and ask for wisdom. God promises to give it liberally (James 1:5). He who gets wisdom loves his own soul (Proverbs 19:8). If you have wisdom, you will think right, do right, and speak right. Remember: He who wins souls is wise (Proverbs 11:30).

14:15 We show our love for God by our obedience. If we do not obey, we do not truly love Him (see vv. 23,24). There are many who call Him "Lord, Lord," but do not do what He says. Matthew 7:21–23 tells us their fearful fate.

14:21 Jesus' unique words: Jesus promises that He and the Father will reveal themselves to all who love and obey Him. This is the ultimate challenge to any skeptic. See John 17:5 comment.

Questions & Objections

14:21 *"I made a commitment, but nothing happened."*

Some people don't get past "square one" because they trust in their feelings rather than God. His promises are true, despite our feelings. If I make a promise to my wife, that promise is true whether she is feeling happy or sad. If she doubts my word, then she brings a slur to my integrity.

Anyone who genuinely repents and trusts in Christ will be saved. The Bible makes this promise: "He that has my commandments, and keeps them, he it is that loves me: and he that loves me shall be loved of my Father, and I will love him, and will manifest myself to him" [John 14:21]. There's the promise, and there's the condition. Any person who loves and obeys Jesus will begin a supernatural relationship with Him and the Father. He said, "And this is life eternal, that they might know you the only true God, and Jesus Christ, whom you have sent" (John 17:3). That doesn't mean you will hear voices or see visions. God will instead make you a new person from within. He will send His Spirit to live within you. You will have a new heart with new desires. You will suddenly become conscious of God and His creation. The Bible will open up to you and become a living Word, and you will have an inner witness that you are saved, that your name is written in heaven, and that death has lost its sting (1 John 5:10–12).

30 Hereafter I will not talk much with you: for the prince of this world comes, and has nothing in me.

31 But that the world may know that I love the Father; and as the Father gave me commandment, even so I do. Arise, let us go hence.

Chapter 15

I am the true vine, and my Father is the husbandman.

2 Every branch in me that bears not fruit he takes away: and every branch that bears fruit, he purges it, that it may bring forth more fruit.

3 Now you are clean through the word which I have spoken to you.

4 Abide in me, and I in you. As the branch cannot bear fruit of itself, except it abide in the vine; no more can you, except you abide in me.

5   I am the vine, you are the branches: He that abides in me, and I in him, the same brings forth much fruit: for without me you can do nothing.

6   If a man abide not in me, he is cast forth as a branch, and is withered; and men gather them, and cast them into the fire, and they are burned.

7   If you abide in me, and my words abide in you, you shall ask what you will, and it shall be done to you.

8   Herein is my Father glorified, that you bear much fruit; so shall you be my disciples.

9   As the Father has loved me, so have I loved you: continue in my love.

10   If you keep my commandments, you shall abide in my love; even as I have kept my Father's commandments, and abide in his love.

> "There must be true and deep conviction of sin. This the preacher must labor to produce, for where this is not felt, the new birth has not taken place."
>
> Charles Spurgeon

11   These things have I spoken to you, that my joy might remain in you, and that your joy might be full.

12   This is my commandment, That you love one another, as I have loved you.

13   Greater love has no man than this, that a man lay down his life for his friends.

14   You are my friends, if you do whatsoever I command you.

15   Henceforth I call you not servants; for the servant knows not what his lord does: but I have called you friends; for all things that I have heard of my Father I have made known to you.

16   You have not chosen me, but I have chosen you, and ordained you, that you should go and bring forth fruit, and that your fruit should remain: that whatsoever you shall ask of the Father in my name, he may give it you.

17   These things I command you, that you love one another.

18   If the world hate you, you know that it hated me before it hated you.

15:18–21 Some preachers promise a life of peace and happiness, but the Bible promises something else: "all that will live godly in Christ Jesus shall suffer persecution" (2 Timothy 3:12). See Matthew 10:16 and Philippians 1:29 comments.

Springboards for Preaching and Witnessing

15:13 *Revolting Natives*

An African chief got wind of a mutiny being planned in his tribe. In an effort to quash the revolt, he called the tribe together and said that anyone caught in rebellion would be given one hundred lashes, without mercy.

A short time later, to the chief's dismay he found that his own brother was behind the revolt. He was trying to overthrow him so he could be head of the tribe. Everyone thought the chief would break his word. But being a just man, he had his brother tied to a tree. Then he had himself tied next to him, and he took those one hundred lashes across his own bare flesh, in his brother's place. In doing so, he not only kept his word (justice was done), but he also demonstrated his great love and forgiveness toward his brother.

19 If you were of the world, the world would love his own: but because you are not of the world, but I have chosen you out of the world, therefore the world hates you.

20 Remember the word that I said to you, The servant is not greater than his lord. If they have persecuted me, they will also persecute you; if they have kept my saying, they will keep yours also.

21 But all these things will they do to you for my name's sake, because they know not him that sent me.

22 If I had not come and spoken to them, they had not had sin: but now they have no cloak for their sin.

23 He that hates me hates my Father also.

24 If I had not done among them the works which none other man did, they had not had sin: but now have they both seen and hated both me and my Father.

25 But this comes to pass, that the word might be fulfilled that is written in their law, They hated me without a cause.

26 But when the Comforter is come, whom I will send to you from the Father, even the Spirit of truth, which proceeds from the Father, he shall testify of me:

27 And you also shall bear witness, because you have been with me from the beginning.

Chapter 16

These things have I spoken to you, that you should not be offended. 2 They shall put you out of the synagogues: yea, the time comes, that whosoever kills you will think that he does God service.

3   And these things will they do to you, because they have not known the Father, nor me.

4   But these things have I told you, that when the time shall come, you may remember that I told you of them. And these things I said not to you at the beginning, because I was with you.

5   But now I go my way to him that sent me; and none of you asks me, Where are you going?

6   But because I have said these things to you, sorrow has filled your heart.

7   Nevertheless I tell you the truth; It is expedient for you that I go away: for if I go not away, the Comforter will not come to you; but if I depart, I will send him to you.

8   And when he is come, he will reprove the world of sin, and of righteousness, and of judgment:

16:8–11 The Holy Spirit's role in salvation. The question may arise about the Holy Spirit's role in the salvation of sinners. The answer is clear from Scripture. We are drawn by, convicted by, born of, and kept by the Holy Spirit. Why then do we need to use the Law when witnessing? Why don't we just leave the salvation of sinners up to the Holy Spirit? Simply because, just as God has condescended to choose the foolishness of preaching to save those who believe, so He has chosen the Moral Law to bring the knowledge of sin.

Jesus Himself tells us how the Holy Spirit works in the salvation of the lost. He said that when the Holy Spirit comes "he will reprove the world of sin [which is transgression of the Law—1 John 3:4], and of righteousness [which is of the Law—Romans 8:4], and of judgment [which is by the Law—Romans 2:12]." So when we use the Law to bring the knowledge of sin to the lost, we simply become instruments the Holy Spirit uses to lead sinners to the Savior.

"When 100 years ago earnest scholars decreed that the Law had no relationship to the preaching of the gospel, they deprived the Holy Spirit in the area where their influence prevailed of the only instrument with which He had ever armed Himself to prepare sinners for grace." Paris Reidhead

"The Holy Spirit convicts us...He shows us the Ten Commandments; the Law is the schoolmaster that leads us to Christ. We look in the mirror of the Ten Commandments, and we see ourselves in that mirror." Billy Graham

9 Of sin, because they believe not on me;

10 Of righteousness, because I go to my Father, and you see me no more;

11 Of judgment, because the prince of this world is judged.

12 I have yet many things to say to you, but you cannot bear them now.

13 Howbeit when he, the Spirit of truth, is come, he will guide you into all truth: for he shall not speak of himself; but whatsoever he shall hear, that shall he speak: and he will show you things to come.

14 He shall glorify me: for he shall receive of mine, and shall show it to you.

15 All things that the Father has are mine: therefore said I, that he shall take of mine, and shall show it to you.

16 A little while, and you shall not see me: and again, a little while, and you shall see me, because I go to the Father.

17 Then said some of his disciples among themselves, What is this that he said to us, A little while, and you shall not see me: and again, a little while, and you shall see me: and, Because I go to the Father?

18 They said therefore, What is this that he says, A little while? we cannot tell what he says.

19 Now Jesus knew that they were desirous to ask him, and said to them, Do you inquire among yourselves of that I said, A little while, and you shall not see me: and again, a little while, and you shall see me?

16:9 Why will sinners go to hell? Much damage has been done to the cause of the gospel by telling the world that they will go to hell "because they don't believe in Jesus." This makes no sense to the ungodly. It seems unreasonable that God would eternally damn them for not believing something. However, the verse can be explained this way: If a man jumps out of a plane without a parachute, he will perish because he transgressed the law of gravity. Had he put on a parachute, he would have been saved. In one sense, he perished because he didn't put on the parachute. But the primary reason he died was because he broke the law of gravity.

If a sinner refuses to trust in Jesus Christ when he passes through the door of death, he will perish. This isn't because he refused to trust the Savior, but because he transgressed the Law of God. Had he "put on the Lord Jesus Christ" (Romans 13:14), he would have been saved; but because he refused to repent, he will suffer the full consequences of his sin. Sin is not "failing to believe in Jesus." Sin is "transgression of the Law" (1 John 3:4).

20 Verily, verily, I say to you, That you shall weep and lament, but the world shall rejoice: and you shall be sorrowful, but your sorrow shall be turned into joy.

21 A woman when she is in travail has sorrow, because her hour is come: but as soon as she is delivered of the child, she remembers no more the anguish, for joy that a man is born into the world.

22 And you now therefore have sorrow: but I will see you again, and your heart shall rejoice, and your joy no man takes from you.

23 And in that day you shall ask me nothing. Verily, verily, I say to you, Whatsoever you shall ask the Father in my name, he will give it you.

24 Hitherto have you asked nothing in my name: ask, and you shall receive, that your joy may be full.

25 These things have I spoken to you in proverbs: but the time comes, when I shall no more speak to you in proverbs, but I shall show you plainly of the Father.

26 At that day you shall ask in my name: and I say not to you, that I will pray the Father for you:

27 For the Father himself loves you, because you have loved me, and have believed that I came out from God.

28 I came forth from the Father, and am come into the world: again, I leave the world, and go to the Father.

29 His disciples said to him, Lo, now you speak plainly, and speak no proverb.

30 Now are we sure that you know all things, and need not that any man should ask you; by this we believe that you came forth from God.

31 Jesus answered them, Do you now believe?

32 Behold, the hour comes, yea, is now come, that you shall be scattered, every man to his own, and shall leave me alone: and yet I am not alone, because the Father is with me.

33 These things I have spoken to you, that in me you might have peace. In the world you shall have tribulation: but be of good cheer; I have overcome the world.

Chapter 17

These words spoke Jesus, and lifted up his eyes to heaven, and said, Father, the hour is come; glorify your Son, that your Son also may glorify you:

Questions & Objections

17:3 *"I don't believe that God is knowable."*

It is amazing how it's human nature to assume that because we believe or don't believe something, that makes it true. Some may not believe in the law of gravity, and may feel they have "evidence" to back up their belief. However, gravity exists whether they believe in it or not. The truth is, God is knowable. Jesus testified, "And this is life eternal, that they might know you the only true God, and Jesus Christ, whom you have sent" (John 17:3). We not only have the testimony of the Scriptures to tell us this, but we have the testimony of multitudes of Christians who know the Lord personally. It is more truthful to say, "I don't want to know God." Sinful man runs from Him as did Adam in the garden of Eden.

2   As you have given him power over all flesh, that he should give eternal life to as many as you have given him.

3   And this is life eternal, that they might know you the only true God, and Jesus Christ, whom you have sent.

4   I have glorified you on the earth: I have finished the work which you gave me to do.

5   And now, O Father, glorify me with your own self with the glory which I had with you before the world was.

6   I have manifested your name to the men which you gave me out of the world: yours they were, and you gave them me; and they have kept your word.

7   Now they have known that all things whatsoever you have given me are of you.

8   For I have given to them the words which you gave me; and they have received them, and have known surely that I came out from you, and they have believed that you did send me.

9   I pray for them: I pray not for the world, but for them which you have given me; for they are yours.

10   And all mine are yours, and yours are mine; and I am glorified in them.

11   And now I am no more in the world, but these are in the world, and I come to you. Holy Father, keep through your own name those whom you have given me, that they may be one, as we are.

12   While I was with them in the world, I kept them in your name: those that you gave me I have kept, and none of them is lost, but the son of perdition; that the scripture might be fulfilled.

Springboards for Preaching and Witnessing

17:3 *Experiential Faith*

Our faith isn't intellectual; it is experiential. We don't know about God, we know Him. At the University of Chicago Divinity School, each year they have what is called "Baptist Day." It is a day when the school invites all the Baptists in the area to the school because they want the Baptist dollars to keep coming in.

On this day each one is to bring a lunch to be eaten outdoors in a grassy picnic area. Every "Baptist Day" the school would invite one of the greatest minds to lecture in the theological education center. One year they invited Dr. Paul Tillich. Dr. Tillich spoke for two-and-a-half hours proving that the resurrection of Jesus was false. He quoted scholar after scholar and book after book. He concluded that since there was no such thing as the historical resurrection, the religious tradition of the Church was groundless, emotional mumbo-jumbo, because it was based on a relationship with a risen Jesus, who, in fact, never rose from the dead in any literal sense. He then asked if there were any questions.

After about 30 seconds, an old preacher with a head of short-cropped, woolly white hair stood up in the back of the auditorium. "Docta Tillich, I got one question," he said as all eyes turned toward him. He reached into his lunch sack and pulled out an apple and began eating it. "Docta Tillich (crunch, munch), my question is a simple one (crunch, munch). Now, I ain't never read them books you read (crunch, munch), and I can't recite the Scriptures in the original Greek (crunch, munch). I don't know nothin' about Niebuhr and Heidegger (crunch, munch)." He finished the apple. "All I wanna know is: This apple I just ate — was it bitter or sweet?"

Dr. Tillich paused for a moment and answered in exemplary scholarly fashion: "I cannot possibly answer that question, for I haven't tasted your apple." The white-haired preacher dropped the apple core into his crumpled paper bag, looked up at Dr. Tillich and said calmly, "Neither have you tasted my Jesus."

The 1,000-plus in attendance could not contain themselves. The auditorium erupted with applause and cheers. Dr. Tillich thanked his audience and promptly left the platform.

"Taste and see that the Lord is good: blessed is the man that trusts in him" (Psalm 34:8). It has been well said, "The man with an experience is not at the mercy of a man with an argument."

13 And now come I to you; and these things I speak in the world, that they might have my joy fulfilled in themselves.

14 I have given them your word; and the world has hated them, because they are not of the world, even as I am not of the world.

15 I pray not that you should take them out of the world, but that you should keep them from the evil.

16 They are not of the world, even as I am not of the world.

17 Sanctify them through your truth: your word is truth.

18 As you have sent me into the world, even so have I also sent them into the world.

17:14 Do you feel discouraged by negative reactions to the gospel? You shouldn't. According to the Gospels, the religious leaders tried to kill Jesus ten times. Let's look to Scripture and see what happened when Paul preached the biblical gospel:

Acts 13:45: The crowd began "contradicting and blaspheming."

Acts 13:50: Paul and Barnabas were persecuted and thrown out of the region.

Acts 14:5: The crowd plotted to stone them, forcing them to flee.

Acts 14:19: Paul was stoned and left for dead.

Acts 16:23: Both Paul and Silas were beaten with "many stripes" and thrown in prison.

Acts 18:6: Paul's hearers "opposed themselves, and blasphemed."

Acts 19:26–28: His hearers were "full of wrath" and seized Paul's companions.

Acts 20:23: The Holy Spirit warned Paul that bonds and afflictions awaited him wherever he preached the gospel.

Acts 22:21,22: His listeners called for his death.

Acts 23:1,2: As soon as he began to speak, he was smacked in the mouth.

Acts 23:10. After Paul spoke there was "great dissension" in the crowd and he was nearly "pulled in pieces."

Acts 23:12,13: More than forty Jews conspired to murder him.

Acts 24:5: He is called a "pestilent fellow," a "mover of sedition," and a "ringleader" of a "sect."

17:22 Was Jesus God in human form? See Colossians 1:15,16.

19 And for their sakes I sanctify myself, that they also might be sanctified through the truth.

20 Neither pray I for these alone, but for them also which shall believe on me through their word;

21 That they all may be one; as you, Father, are in me, and I in you, that they also may be one in us: that the world may believe that you have sent me.

22 And the glory which you gave me I have given them; that they may be one, even as we are one:

23 I in them, and you in me, that they may be made perfect in one; and that the world may know that you have sent me, and have loved them, as you have loved me.

24 Father, I will that they also, whom you have given me, be with me where I am; that they may behold my glory, which you have given me: for you loved me before the foundation of the world.

25 O righteous Father, the world has not known you: but I have known you, and these have known that you have sent me.

26 And I have declared to them your name, and will declare it: that the love wherewith you have loved me may be in them, and I in them.

Chapter 18

When Jesus had spoken these words, he went forth with his disciples over the brook Cedron, where was a garden, into the which he entered, and his disciples.

2 And Judas also, which betrayed him, knew the place: for Jesus often resorted there with his disciples.

3 Judas then, having received a band of men and officers from the chief priests and Pharisees, came there with lanterns and torches and weapons.

4 Jesus therefore, knowing all things that should come upon him, went forth, and said to them, Whom do you seek?

5 They answered him, Jesus of Nazareth. Jesus said to them, I am he. And Judas also, which betrayed him, stood with them.

6 As soon then as he had said to them, I am he, they went backward, and fell to the ground.

7 Then asked he them again, Whom do you seek? And they said, Jesus of Nazareth.

8 Jesus answered, I have told you that I am he: if therefore you seek me, let these go their way:

9   That the saying might be fulfilled, which he spoke, Of them which you gave me have I lost none.

10   Then Simon Peter having a sword drew it, and smote the high priest's servant, and cut off his right ear. The servant's name was Malchus.

11   Then said Jesus to Peter, Put up your sword into the sheath: the cup which my Father has given me, shall I not drink it?

12   Then the band and the captain and officers of the Jews took Jesus, and bound him,

13   And led him away to Annas first; for he was father in law to Caiaphas, which was the high priest that same year.

14   Now Caiaphas was he, which gave counsel to the Jews, that it was expedient that one man should die for the people.

15   And Simon Peter followed Jesus, and so did another disciple: that disciple was known to the high priest, and went in with Jesus into the palace of the high priest.

16   But Peter stood at the door without. Then went out that other disciple, which was known to the high priest, and spoke to her that kept the door, and brought in Peter.

17   Then said the damsel that kept the door to Peter, are you not also one of this man's disciples? He said, I am not.

18   And the servants and officers stood there, who had made a fire of coals; for it was cold: and they warmed themselves: and Peter stood with them, and warmed himself

19   The high priest then asked Jesus of his disciples, and of his doctrine.

20   Jesus answered him, I spoke openly to the world; I ever taught in the synagogue, and in the temple, where the Jews always resort; and in secret have I said nothing.

21   Why do you ask me? ask them which heard me, what I have said to them: behold, they know what I said.

22   And when he had thus spoken, one of the officers which stood by struck Jesus with the palm of his hand, saying, Do you answer the high priest so?

23   Jesus answered him, If I have spoken evil, bear witness of the evil: but if well, why do you smite me?

24   Now Annas had sent him bound to Caiaphas the high priest.

18:17   Who of us who know the Lord cannot identify with Peter? We have felt the paralyzing power of the fear of man grip our hearts and fasten our lips. Peter stood by the fire and warmed his cold body, but what he really needed was a fiery coal from the altar of God to touch his frozen lips.

25 And Simon Peter stood and warmed himself. They said therefore to him, are not you also one of his disciples? He denied it, and said, I am not.

26 One of the servants of the high priest, being his kinsman whose ear Peter cut off, said, Did not I see you in the garden with him?

27 Peter then denied again: and immediately the cock crew.

28 Then led they Jesus from Caiaphas to the hall of judgment: and it was early; and they themselves went not into the judgment hall, lest they should be defiled; but that they might eat the passover.

29 Pilate then went out to them, and said, What accusation do you bring against this man?

30 They answered and said to him, If he were not a malefactor, we would not have delivered him up to you.

31 Then said Pilate to them, You take him, and judge him according to your law. The Jews therefore said to him, It is not lawful for us to put any man to death:

32 That the saying of Jesus might be fulfilled, which he spoke, signifying what death he should die.

33 Then Pilate entered into the judgment hall again, and called Jesus, and said to him, Are you the King of the Jews?

34 Jesus answered him, Do you say this thing of yourself, or did others tell it of me?

35 Pilate answered, Am I a Jew? Your own nation and the chief priests have delivered you to me: what have you done?

36 Jesus answered, My kingdom is not of this world: if my kingdom were of this world, then would my servants fight, that I should not be delivered to the Jews: but now is my kingdom not from hence.

37 Pilate therefore said to him, Are you a king then? Jesus answered, You say that I am a king. To this end was I born, and for this cause came I into the world, that I should bear witness to the truth. Every one that is of the truth hears my voice.

38 Pilate said to him, What is truth? And when he had said this, he went out again to the Jews, and said to them, I find in him no fault at all.

39 But you have a custom, that I should release to you one at the passover: will you therefore that I release to you the King of the Jews?

40 Then cried they all again, saying, Not this man, but Barabbas. Now Barabbas was a robber.

Chapter 19

Then Pilate therefore took Jesus, and scourged him.

2 And the soldiers platted a crown of thorns, and put it on his head, and they put on him a purple robe,

3 And said, Hail, King of the Jews! and they smote him with their hands.

4 Pilate therefore went forth again, and said to them, Behold, I bring him forth to you, that you may know that I find no fault in him.

5 Then came Jesus forth, wearing the crown of thorns, and the purple robe. And Pilate said to them, Behold the man!

6 When the chief priests therefore and officers saw him, they cried out, saying, Crucify him, crucify him. Pilate said to them, You take him, and crucify him: for I find no fault in him.

7 The Jews answered him, We have a law, and by our law he ought to die, because he made himself the Son of God.

8 When Pilate therefore heard that saying, he was the more afraid;

9 And went again into the judgment hall, and said to Jesus, Where are you from? But Jesus gave him no answer.

10 Then said Pilate to him, Do you not speak to me? Do you not know that I have power to crucify you, and have power to release you?

11 Jesus answered, You could have no power at all against me, except it were given you from above: therefore he that delivered me to you has the greater sin.

12 And from thenceforth Pilate sought to release him: but the Jews cried out, saying, If you let this man go, you are not Caesar's friend: whosoever makes himself a king speaks against Caesar.

13 When Pilate therefore heard that saying, he brought Jesus forth, and sat down in the judgment seat in a place that is called the Pavement, but in the Hebrew, Gabbatha.

14 And it was the preparation of the passover, and about the sixth hour: and he said to the Jews, Behold your King!

19:1,2 It was plain that the direction this Pilate was taking was not a good one, and he knew it. He could see that it was going to land him on ground he preferred not to touch. He tried vainly to alter his course by having Jesus scourged, in the hope that it would appease the Jews. After the whipping, the twisted soldiers twisted a crown of thorns and put it on His head. This was perhaps symbolic of the Messiah taking upon Himself the curse placed upon creation when Adam sinned (Genesis 3:18).

15 But they cried out, Away with him, away with him, crucify him. Pilate said to them, Shall I crucify your King? The chief priest answered, We have no king but Caesar.

16 Then delivered he him therefore to them to be crucified. And they took Jesus, and led him away.

17 And he bearing his cross went forth into a place called the place of a skull, which is called in the Hebrew Golgotha:

18 Where they crucified him, and two other with him, on either side one, and Jesus in the midst.

19 And Pilate wrote a title, and put it on the cross. And the writing was, JESUS OF NAZARETH THE KING OF THE JEWS.

20 This title then read many of the Jews: for the place where Jesus was crucified was near to the city: and it was written in Hebrew, and Greek, and Latin.

21 Then said the chief priests of the Jews to Pilate, Write not, The King of the Jews; but that he said, I am King of the Jews.

22 Pilate answered, What I have written I have written.

23 Then the soldiers, when they had crucified Jesus, took his garments, and made four parts, to every soldier a part; and also his coat: now the coat was without seam, woven from the top throughout.

24 They said therefore among themselves, Let us not rend it, but cast lots for it, whose it shall be: that the scripture might be fulfilled, which says, They parted my raiment among them, and for my vesture they did cast lots. These things therefore the soldiers did.

25 Now there stood by the cross of Jesus his mother, and his mother's sister, Mary the wife of Cleophas, and Mary Magdalene.

19:29 Messianic prophecy fulfilled: "They gave me also gall for my meat; and in my thirst they gave me vinegar to drink." (Psalm 69:21). See John 19:33,36 comment.

19:31,32 Archeology confirms the Bible. "During the past four decades, spectacular discoveries have produced data corroborating the historical backdrop of the Gospels. In 1968, for example, the skeletal remains of a crucified man were found in a burial cave in northern Jerusalem ... There was evidence that his wrists may have been pierced with nails. The knees had been doubled up and turned sideways and an iron nail (still lodged in the heel bone of one foot) driven through both heels. The shinbones appeared to have been broken, perhaps corroborating the Gospel of John." Jeffery L. Sheler, "Is the Bible True?" Reader's Digest, June 2000

26 When Jesus therefore saw his mother, and the disciple standing by, whom he loved, he said to his mother, Woman, behold your son!

27 Then said he to the disciple, Behold your mother! And from that hour that disciple took her to his own home.

28 After this, Jesus knowing that all things were now accomplished, that the scripture might be fulfilled, said, I thirst.

29 Now there was set a vessel full of vinegar: and they filled a sponge with vinegar, and put it upon hyssop, and put it to his mouth.

30 When Jesus therefore had received the vinegar, he said, It is finished: and he bowed his head, and gave up the ghost.

31 The Jews therefore, because it was the preparation, that the bodies should not remain upon the cross on the sabbath day, (for that sabbath day was an high day,) besought Pilate that their legs might be broken, and that they might be taken away.

32 Then came the soldiers, and broke the legs of the first, and of the other which was crucified with him.

33 But when they came to Jesus, and saw that he was dead already, they broke not his legs:

34 But one of the soldiers with a spear pierced his side, and forthwith came there out blood and water.

35 And he that saw it bare record, and his record is true: and he knows what he said is true, that you might believe.

36 For these things were done, that the scripture should be fulfilled, A bone of him shall not be broken.

37 And again another scripture says, They shall look on him whom they pierced.

38 And after this Joseph of Arimathaea, being a disciple of Jesus, but secretly for fear of the Jews, besought Pilate that he might take away

---

19:33,34 "Clearly the weight of historical and medical evidence indicates that Jesus was dead before the wound to His side was inflicted and supports the traditional view that the spear, thrust between his right rib, probably perforated not only the right lung but also the pericardium and heart and thereby ensured His death. Accordingly, interpretations based on the assumption that Jesus did not die on the cross appear to be at odds with modern medical knowledge." Journal of the American Medical Society, March 21, 1986

19:33,36 Messianic prophecy fulfilled: As Exodus 12:46 instructs, none of the Passover lamb's bones were to be broken. When Jesus, our Passover Lamb, was sacrificed for our sins, none of His bones were broken.

Questions & Objections

19:33,34 *"Is it possible that Jesus simply fainted on the cross, and revived while He was in the tomb?"*

Jesus had been whipped and beaten, and was bleeding from His head, back, hands, and feet for at least six hours. While he was on the cross, a soldier pierced His side with a spear and blood and water gushed out. Professional soldiers would certainly have completed their assigned task and ensured his death.

"It is impossible that a being who had stolen half-dead out of the sepulcher, who crept about weak and ill, wanting medical treatment, who required bandaging, strengthening, and indulgence, and who still at last yielded to his sufferings, could have given to the disciples the impression that he was a conqueror over death and the grave, the Prince of Life: an impression which lay at the bottom of their future ministry. Such a resuscitation could only have weakened the impression which he had made upon them in life and in death, at the most could only have given it an elegiac voice, but could by no possibility have changed their sorrow into enthusiasm, have elevated their reverence into worship." Strauss, New Life of Jesus (quoted in Who Moved the Stone? by Frank Morison)

the body of Jesus: and Pilate gave him leave. He came therefore, and took the body of Jesus.

39 And there came also Nicodemus, which at the first came to Jesus by night, and brought a mixture of myrrh and aloes, about an hundred pound weight.

40 Then took they the body of Jesus, and wound it in linen clothes with the spices, as the manner of the Jews is to bury.

41 Now in the place where he was crucified there was a garden; and in the garden a new sepulchre, wherein was never man yet laid.

42 There laid they Jesus therefore because of the Jews' preparation day; for the sepulchre was near at hand.

Chapter 20

The first day of the week came Mary Magdalene early, when it was yet dark, to the sepulchre, and saw the stone taken away from the sepulchre.

2 Then she ran, and came to Simon Peter, and to the other disciple, whom Jesus loved, and said to them, They have taken away the Lord out of the sepulchre, and we know not where they have laid him.

3 Peter therefore went forth, and that other disciple, and came to the sepulchre.

4 So they ran both together: and the other disciple did outrun Peter, and came first to the sepulchre.

5 And he stooping down, and looking in, saw the linen clothes lying; yet went he not in.

6 Then came Simon Peter following him, and went into the sepulchre, and saw the linen clothes lie,

7 And the napkin, that was about his head, not lying with the linen clothes, but wrapped together in a place by itself.

8 Then went in also that other disciple, which came first to the sepulchre, and he saw, and believed.

9 For as yet they knew not the scripture, that he must rise again from the dead.

10 Then the disciples went away again to their own home.

11 But Mary stood without at the sepulchre weeping: and as she wept, she stooped down, and looked into the sepulchre,

12 And saw two angels in white sitting, the one at the head, and the other at the feet, where the body of Jesus had lain.

13 And they said to her, Woman, why are you weeping? She said to them, Because they have taken away my Lord, and I know not where they have laid him.

14 And when she had thus said, she turned herself back, and saw Jesus standing, and knew not that it was Jesus.

15 Jesus said to her, Woman, why are you weeping? whom do you seek? She, supposing him to be the gardener, said to him, Sir, if you have borne him hence, tell me where you have laid him, and I will take him away.

16 Jesus said to her, Mary. She turned herself, and said to him, Rabboni; which is to say, Master.

17 Jesus said to her, Touch me not; for I am not yet ascended to my Father: but go to my brethren, and say to them, I ascend to my Father, and your Father; and to my God, and your God.

18 Mary Magdalene came and told the disciples that she had seen the Lord, and that he had spoken these things to her.

19 Then the same day at evening, being the first day of the week, when the doors were shut where the disciples were assembled for

fear of the Jews, came Jesus and stood in the midst, and said to them, Peace be to you.

20 And when he had so said, he showed to them his hands and his side. Then were the disciples glad, when they saw the Lord.

21 Then said Jesus to them again, Peace be to you: as my Father has sent me, even so send I you.

22 And when he had said this, he breathed on them, and said to them, Receive the Holy Spirit:

23 Whose soever sins you remit, they are remitted to them; and whose soever sins you retain, they are retained.

24 But Thomas, one of the twelve, called Didymus, was not with them when Jesus came.

25 The other disciples therefore said to him, We have seen the Lord. But he said to them, Except I shall see in his hands the print of the nails, and put my finger into the print of the nails, and thrust my hand into his side, I will not believe.

20:18 The first evangelist was a woman. She took the good news of the resurrection to the men, who were hiding behind locked doors.

20:22 Why did Jesus breathe on His disciples and say, "Receive the Holy Spirit," when He had already told them that the Holy Spirit could come only after His ascension (John 16:7)? Perhaps it was at that moment that the Body of Christ on earth was conceived within the womb. Perhaps it was then that He planted the seed of the life of the Church, but after the gestation period, on the Day of Pentecost, the Body of Christ was then birthed on earth.

The first seed of Adam's race began with the breath of God (Genesis 2:7), but the "last Adam" began with the breath of God in Christ. The first man had been formed from the dust of the ground, and when the Lord God breathed into his nostrils the breath of life, he became a "living soul," but Christ was made a "quickening spirit" (1 Corinthians 15:45).

Jesus picked up fallen dust from the ground of Israel, shaped them for three years, and now He breathed life into them, as He did in Genesis with the dust He had formed into Adam's body. It was but a gentle breath at conception, which became a rushing mighty wind on the Day of Pentecost (Acts 2:2), and caused the living Body of Christ to stand on its feet on earth.

20:23 If someone has turned from sin and is trusting in Jesus Christ alone for his eternal salvation, every believer has power to inform him that his sin is forgiven, based on his professed faith in the Savior

26 And after eight days again his disciples were within, and Thomas with them: then came Jesus, the doors being shut, and stood in the midst, and said, Peace be to you.

27 Then said he to Thomas, reach here your finger, and behold my hands; and reach here your hand, and thrust it into my side: and be not faithless, but believing.

28 And Thomas answered and said to him, My Lord and my God.

29 Jesus said to him, Thomas, because you have seen me, you have believed: blessed are they that have not seen, and yet have believed.

30 And many other signs truly did Jesus in the presence of his disciples, which are not written in this book:

31 But these are written, that you might believe that Jesus is the Christ, the Son of God; and that believing you might have life through his name.

Chapter 21

After these things Jesus showed himself again to the disciples at the sea of Tiberias; and on this wise showed he himself.

20:26 Scientific Facts in the Bible. Babies are circumcised on the eighth day because this is the day that the coagulating factor in the blood, called prothrombin, is the highest. Medical science has discovered that this is when the human body's immune system is at its peak.

Just as the eighth day was the God-given timing for circumcision (Genesis 17:12), there is a God-given timing for every person who is "circumcised with the circumcision made without hands" (Colossians 2:11). Jesus appeared to Thomas on the eighth day. What Thomas saw cut away the flesh of his unbelieving heart. He became a Jew inwardly as his circumcision became "that of the heart, in the spirit, and not in the letter" (Romans 2:29). Thomas bowed his heart to Jesus of Nazareth as his Lord and his God. He needed a miracle, and God graciously gave it to him.

Each of us is dealt with individually by God; some get incredible spiritual manifestations at conversion. Others quietly trust the promises of God, and God reveals Himself to them through faith rather than feelings of great joy. What matters is not how each of us came to Christ, but that we became new creatures in Christ, because that is the real miracle that proves the reality of salvation. This is what Paul meant when he wrote, "For in Christ Jesus neither circumcision avails anything, nor uncircumcision, but a new creature" (Galatians 6:15).

Questions & Objections

20:25   *"Seeing is believeing. If I can't see it, I don't believe it exists."*

We believe in many things that we can't see. Ask a skeptic if he has ever seen the wind. Has he seen history? Has he ever seen his brain? We see the effects of the wind, but the wind is invisible. We have records of history, but it is by "faith" that we believe certain historical events happened. Television waves are invisible, but an antenna and a receiver can detect their presence. The unregenerate man likewise has a "receiver." However, the receiver (his spirit) is dead because of sin (Ephesians 2:1). He needs to be plugged into the life of God; then he will come alive and be aware of the invisible spiritual realm.

2　There were together Simon Peter, and Thomas called Didymus, and Nathanael of Cana in Galilee, and the sons of Zebedee, and two other of his disciples.

3　Simon Peter said to them, I go a fishing. They said to him, We also go with you. They went forth, and entered into a ship immediately; and that night they caught nothing.

4　But when the morning was now come, Jesus stood on the shore: but the disciples knew not that it was Jesus.

5　Then Jesus said to them, Children, have you any meat? They answered him, No.

6　And he said to them, Cast the net on the right side of the ship, and you shall find. They cast therefore, and now they were not able to draw it for the multitude of fishes.

7　Therefore that disciple whom Jesus loved said to Peter, It is the Lord. Now when Simon Peter heard that it was the Lord, he girt his fisher's coat to him, (for he was naked,) and did cast himself into the sea.

8　And the other disciples came in a little ship; (for they were not far from land, but as it were two hundred cubits,) dragging the net with fishes.

9　As soon then as they were come to land, they saw a fire of coals there, and fish laid thereon, and bread.

10　Jesus said to them, Bring of the fish which you have now caught.

11　Simon Peter went up, and drew the net to land full of great fishes, an hundred and fifty and three: and for all there were so many, yet was not the net broken.

12 Jesus said to them, Come and dine. And none of the disciples dared ask him, Who are you? knowing that it was the Lord.

13 Jesus then came, and took bread, and gave, and fish likewise.

14 This is now the third time that Jesus showed himself to his disciples, after that he was risen from the dead.

15 So when they had dined, Jesus said to Simon Peter, Simon, son of Jonah, do you love me more than these? He said to him, Yea, Lord; you know that I love you. He said to him, Feed my lambs.

16 He said to him again the second time, Simon, son of Jonah, do you love me? He said to him, Yea, Lord; you know that I love you. He said to him, Feed my sheep.

17 He said to him the third time, Simon, son of Jonah, do you love me? Peter was grieved because he said to him the third time, Do you love me? And he said to him, Lord, you know all things; you know that I love you. Jesus said to him, Feed my sheep.

18 Verily, verily, I say to you, When you were young, you girded yourself, and walked where you would: but when you shall be old, you shall stretch forth your hands, and another shall gird you, and carry you where you would not.

19 This spoke he, signifying by what death he should glorify God. And when he had spoken this, he said to him, Follow me.

20 Then Peter, turning about, saw the disciple whom Jesus loved following; which also leaned on his breast at supper, and said, Lord, which is he that betrays you?

"Let men of science and learning expound their knowledge and prize and probe with their researches every detail of the records which have been preserved to us from those dim ages. All they will do is fortify the grand simplicity and essential accuracy of the recorded truths which have lighted so far the pilgrimage of men."

Winston Churchill

21 Peter seeing him said to Jesus, Lord, and what shall this man do?
22 Jesus said to him, If I will that he tarry till I come, what is that
to you? You follow me.
23 Then went this saying abroad among the brethren, that that
disciple should not die: yet Jesus said not to him, He shall not die;
but, If I will that he tarry till I come, what is that to you?
24 This is the disciple which testifies of these things, and wrote these
things: and we know that his testimony is true.
25 And there are also many other things which Jesus did, the which,
if they should be written every one, I suppose that even the world
itself could not contain the books that should be written. Amen.

Islam

OFFICIAL NAME: Islam

KEY FIGURE IN HISTORY: Muhammad (a.d. 570–632)

DATE OF ITS ESTABLISHMENT: a.d. 622

ADHERENTS: Worldwide: Estimated 800 million to 1 billion; 58 percent live in South and Southeast Asia; 28 percent in Africa; 9 percent in Near and Middle East; 5 percent other. U.S.: Estimated 6.5 to 8 million.

WHAT IS ISLAM?

Islam is the world's youngest major world religion. It claims to be the restoration of original monotheism and truth and thus supersedes both Judaism and Christianity. It stresses submission to Allah, the Arabic name for God, and conformity to the "five pillars" or disciplines of that religion as essential for salvation. From its inception, Islam was an aggressively missionary-oriented religion. Within one century of its formation, and often using military force, Islam had spread across the Middle East, most of North Africa, and as far east as India. While God is, in the understanding of most Muslims, unknowable personally, His will is believed to be perfectly revealed in the holy book, the Qur'an. The Qur'an is to be followed completely and its teaching forms a complete guide for life and society.

WHO WAS MUHAMMAD?

Muhammad is believed by Muslims to be the last and greatest prophet of God—"the seal of the prophets." It was through him that the Qur'an was dictated, thus according him the supreme place among the seers of God. A native of Mecca, Muhammad was forced to flee that city in a.d. 622 after preaching vigorously against the paganism of the city. Having secured his leadership in Medina, and with several military victories to his credit, Muhammad returned in triumph to Mecca in a.d. 630. There, he established Islam as the religion of all Arabia.

WHAT IS THE QUR'AN?

The Qur'an is the sacred book of Islam and the perfect word of God for the Muslim. It is claimed that the Qur'an was dictated in Arabic by the angel Gabriel to Muhammad and were God's precise words. As such, it had preexisted from eternity in heaven with God as the "Mother of the Book" and was in that form uncreated and co-eternal with God. Islam teaches that it contains the total and perfect revelation and will of God. The Qur'an is about four-fifths the length of the New Testament and is divided into 114 surahs or chapters. While Islam respects the Torah, the psalms of David, and the four Gospels, the Qur'an stands alone in its authority and absoluteness. It is believed to be most perfectly understood in Arabic and it is a religious obligation to seek to read and quote it in the original language.

WHAT ARE THE "FIVE PILLARS"?

They are the framework for the Muslims' life and discipline. Successful and satisfactory adherence to the pillars satisfies the will of Allah. They form the basis for the Muslim's hope for salvation along with faith and belief in Allah's existence, the authority of Muhammad as a prophet, and the finality and perfection of the Qur'an. The five pillars are:

The confession of Faith or Shahada: It is the declaration that there is no god but Allah and Muhammad is his prophet. Sincerity in the voicing of the confession is necessary for it to be valid. It must be held until death, and repudiation of the Shahada nullifies hope for salvation.

Prayer of Salat: Five times a day, preceded by ceremonial washing, the Muslim is required to pray facing Mecca. Specific formulas recited from the Qur'an (in Arabic), along with prostrations, are included. Prayer is, in this sense, an expression of submission to the will of Allah. While most of Islam has no hierarchical priesthood, prayers are led in mosques by respected lay leaders. The five times of prayer are before sunrise, noon, midafternoon, sunset, and prior to sleep.

Almsgiving or Zakat: The Qur'an teaches the giving of two-and-a-half percent of one's capital wealth to the poor and/or for the propagation of Islam. By doing so, the Muslim's remaining wealth is purified.

The Fast or Sawm: during the course of the lunar month of Ramadan, a fast is to be observed by every Muslim from sunrise to sunset. Nothing is to pass over the lips during this time, and they should refrain from sexual relations. After sunset, feasting and other celebrations often occur. The daylight hours are set aside for self-purification. The month is used to remember the giving of the Qur'an to Muhammad.

Pilgrimage or Hajj: All Muslims who are economically and physically able are required to journey to Mecca at least once in their lifetime. The required simple pilgrim's dress stresses the notion of equality before God. Another element of the Hajj is the mandatory walk of each pilgrim seven times around the Kaabah—the shrine of the black rock, the holiest site of Islam. Muhammad taught that the Kaabah was the original place of worship for Adam and later for Abraham. The Kaabah is thus venerated as the site of true religion, the absolute monotheism of Islam.

THE DOCTRINES OF ISLAM

God: He is numerically and absolutely one. Allah is beyond the understanding of man so that only his will may be revealed and known. He is confessed as the "merciful and compassionate one."

Sin: The most serious sin that can be ascribed to people is that of shirk or considering god as more than one. Original sin is viewed as a "lapse" by Adam. Humankind is considered weak and forgetful but not as fallen.

Angels: Islam affirms the reality of angels as messengers and agents of god. Evil spirits or Jinn also exist. Satan is a fallen angel. Angels perform important functions for Allah both now and at the end of time.

Final Judgment: The world will be judged at the end of time by Allah. The good deeds and obedience of all people to the five pillars and the Qur'an will serve as the basis of judgment.

Salvation: It is determined by faith, as defined by Islam, as well as by compiling good deeds primarily in conformity to the five pillars.

Marriage: Muslims uphold marriage as honorable and condemn adultery. While many Muslim marriages are monogamous, Islamic states allow as many as four wives. Men consider a woman as less than an equal, and while a man has the right to divorce his wife, the wife has no similar power (see Surah 2:228, 4:34).

Nonetheless, the female has a right to own and dispose of property. Modesty in dress is encouraged for both men and women.

War: The term jihad or "struggle" is often considered as both external and internal, both a physical and spiritual struggle. The enemies of Islam or "idolaters," states the Qur'an, may be slain "wherever you find them"

(Surah:5). (See Surah 47:4). Paradise is promised for those who die fighting in the cause of Islam (see Surah 3:195, 2:224). Moderate Muslims emphasize the spiritual dimension of Jihad and not its political element.

ANSWERING MUSLIM OBJECTIONS TO CHRISTIANITY

Christians and Jews are acknowledged as "people of the book," although their failure to conform to the confession of Islam labels them as unbelievers. Following are several questions that Muslims have about Christianity.

Is the Trinity a belief in three gods?

Christians are monotheistic and believe that God is one. But both in His work in accomplishing salvation through the person of Jesus Christ and through biblical study it has become clear that His oneness in fact comprises three persons—Father, Son (Jesus Christ), and the third person of the Godhead, the Holy Spirit. Mary is not part of the Godhead. The notion of God, who is three-in-one, is part of both the mystery and greatness of God. God is in essence one while in persons three. This truth helps us understand God as truly personal and having the capacity to relate to other persons. As well, Christians confirm the holiness, sovereignty, and greatness of God.

How can Jesus be the Son of God?

Scripture affirms that Jesus was conceived supernaturally by the Holy Spirit and was born of the Virgin Mary. It does not in any way claim that Jesus was directly God the Father's biological and physical son. It rejects the notion of the Arabic word for son, walad, meaning physical son, for the word ibin, which is the title of relationship. Jesus is the Son in a symbolic manner designating that He was God the Word who became man in order to save humankind from its sin. The virgin birth was supernatural as God the Holy Spirit conceived in Mary, without physical relations, Jesus the Messiah. In this manner even the Qur'an affirms the miraculous birth of Christ (see Surah 19:16–21). Jesus was in this sense "God's unique Son." During His earthly ministry He carried out the will of the Father. Notably the Qur'an affirms Jesus' supernatural birth, life of miracles, His compassion, and ascension to heaven (see Surah 19:16–21,29–31, 3:37–47, 5:110).

How could Jesus have died on the cross especially if He's God's son?

The testimony of history and the Injil, or the four Gospels, is that Jesus died on the cross. If it is understood that God is love, and that humankind is lost in sin, then is it not likely that God would have provided a sacrifice for sin? Jesus is God's sacrifice for all the sins of the world and is a bridge from a holy God to fallen and sinful humans.

This truth is revealed in the Injil, John 3:16. Even the Qur'an states in Surah 3:55 that "Allah said: O Isa [Jesus], I am going to terminate [to put to death] the period of your stay (on earth) and cause you to ascend unto Me." What other way could this concept have any meaning apart from Jesus' death for sin and His subsequent resurrection?

Muslims believe that God took Jesus from the cross and substituted Judas in His place, or at least someone who looked like Jesus. He was then taken to heaven where He is alive and from where one day He will return.

ANSWERING MUSLIMS' QUESTIONS TO CHRISTIANS ABOUT ISLAM

What do you think about the prophet Muhammad?

Muhammad was apparently a well-meaning man who sought to oppose paganism and evil in his day. While he succeeded in uniting the Arabian Peninsula and upheld several important virtues, we do not believe he received a fresh revelation from God. Jesus Christ fulfilled not only the final prophetic role from God, but He is the Savior or the world and God the Son. While Islam believes that some Bible passages refer to Muhammad (see Deut. 18:18–19; John 14:16; 15:26; 16:7), that is clearly not the meaning of the texts. Other passages may help in understanding and interpreting the previous texts (see Matthew 21:11; Luke 24:19; John 6;14; 7:40; Acts 1:8–16; 7:37).

What is your opinion of the Qur'an?

It is a greatly valued book for the Muslim. It is not received or believed to be a divine book by the Christian. The statements of the Qur'an are accepted only where they agree with the Bible.

What is your opinion about the five pillars?
Salvation is from God and comes only through the saving work of Jesus Christ. When we put our faith in Him, we may be saved (see John 3:16–21,31–36).

WITNESSING TO MUSLIMS
- Be courteous and loving.
- Reflect interest in their beliefs. Allow them time to articulate their views.
- Be acquainted with their basic beliefs.
- Be willing to examine passages of the Qur'an concerning their beliefs.
- Stick to the cardinal doctrines of the Christian faith but also take time to respond to all sincere questions.
- Point out the centrality of the person and work of Jesus Christ for salvation.
- Stress that because of Jesus, His cross, and resurrection, one may have the full assurance of salvation, both now and for eternity (see 1 John 5:13).
- Share the plan of salvation with the Muslim. Point out that salvation is a gift and not to be earned.
- Pray for the fullness of the Holy Spirit. Trust Him to provide wisdom and grace.
- Be willing to become a friend and a personal evangelist to Muslims.

Phil Roberts, Director of Interfaith Evangelism. Copyright 1996 North American Mission Board of the Southern Baptist Convention, Alpharetta, Georgia. All rights reserved. Reprinted with permission.

If you enjoyed The Gospel of John from
The Evidence Bible, you may like to get the whole
Bible from your Christian bookstore.

For a complete selection of books, tracts, DVDs, and CDs
by Ray Comfort (and free resources that you will find
helpful) see www.livingwaters.com.